Motion and Design

TEACHER'S GUIDE

SCIENCE AND TECHNOLOGY FOR CHILDREN

NATIONAL SCIENCE RESOURCES CENTER
Smithsonian Institution • National Academy of Sciences
Arts and Industries Building, Room 1201
Washington, DC 20560

NSRC

The National Science Resources Center is operated by the Smithsonian Institution and the National Academy of Sciences to improve the teaching of science in the nation's schools. The NSRC collects and disseminates information about exemplary teaching resources, develops and disseminates curriculum materials, and sponsors outreach activities, specifically in the areas of leadership development and technical assistance, to help school districts develop and sustain hands-on science programs. The NSRC is located in the Arts and Industries Building of the Smithsonian Institution and in the Capital Gallery Building in Washington, D.C.

STC Project Supporters

National Science Foundation
Smithsonian Institution
U.S. Department of Defense
U.S. Department of Education
John D. and Catherine T. MacArthur Foundation
The Dow Chemical Company Foundation
E. I. du Pont de Nemours & Company
Amoco Foundation, Inc.
Hewlett-Packard Company
Smithsonian Institution Educational Outreach Fund

This project was supported, in part, by the
National Science Foundation
Opinions expressed are those of the authors
and not necessarily those of the Foundation

© 1997 by the National Academy of Sciences. All rights reserved.
01 00 99 98 97   10 9 8 7 6 5 4 3 2 1

ISBN 0-89278-676-0

Published by Carolina Biological Supply Company, 2700 York Road, Burlington, NC 27215.
Call toll free 1-800-334-5551.

No part of this book may be reproduced by any mechanical, photographic, or electronic process, or in the form of a phonographic recording, nor may it be stored in a retrieval system, transmitted, or otherwise copied for public or private use without permission in writing from the National Science Resources Center.

See specific instructions in lessons for photocopying.

This material is based upon work supported by the National Science Foundation under Grant No. ESI-9252947. Any opinions, findings, and conclusions or recommendations expressed in this material are those of the author(s) and do not necessarily reflect the views of the National Science Foundation.

CB787489704

Printed on recycled paper.

Foreword

Since 1988, the National Science Resources Center (NSRC) has been developing Science and Technology for Children (STC), an innovative hands-on science program for children in grades one through six. The 24 units of the STC program, four for each grade level, are designed to provide all students with stimulating experiences in the life, earth, and physical sciences and technology while simultaneously developing their critical-thinking and problem-solving skills.

Sequence of STC Units

Grade	Life, Earth, and Physical Sciences and Technology			
1	Organisms	Weather	Solids and Liquids	Comparing and Measuring
2	The Life Cycle of Butterflies	Soils	Changes	Balancing and Weighing
3	Plant Growth and Development	Rocks and Minerals	Chemical Tests	Sound
4	Animal Studies	Land and Water	Electric Circuits	Motion and Design
5	Microworlds	Ecosystems	Food Chemistry	Floating and Sinking
6	Experiments with Plants	Measuring Time	Magnets and Motors	The Technology of Paper

The STC units provide children with the opportunity to learn age-appropriate concepts and skills and to acquire scientific attitudes and habits of mind. In the primary grades, children begin their study of science by observing, measuring, and identifying properties. Then they move on through a progression of experiences that culminate in grade six with the design of controlled experiments.

Sequence of Development of Scientific Reasoning Skills

Scientific Reasoning Skills	Grades					
	1	2	3	4	5	6
Observing, Measuring, and Identifying Properties	◆	◆	◆	◆	◆	◆
Seeking Evidence Recognizing Patterns and Cycles		◆	◆	◆	◆	◆
Identifying Cause and Effect Extending the Senses				◆	◆	◆
Designing and Conducting Controlled Experiments						◆

The "Focus-Explore-Reflect-Apply" learning cycle incorporated into the STC units is based on research findings about children's learning. These findings indicate that knowledge is actively constructed by each learner and that children learn science best in a hands-on experimental environment where they can make their own discoveries. The steps of the learning cycle are as follows:

- Focus: Explore and clarify the ideas that children already have about the topic.

- Explore: Enable children to engage in hands-on explorations of the objects, organisms, and science phenomena to be investigated.

- Reflect: Encourage children to discuss their observations and to reconcile their ideas.

- Apply: Help children discuss and apply their new ideas in new situations.

The learning cycle in STC units gives students opportunities to develop increased understanding of important scientific concepts and to develop positive attitudes toward science.

The STC units provide teachers with a variety of strategies with which to assess student learning. The STC units also offer teachers opportunities to link the teaching of science with the development of skills in mathematics, language arts, and social studies. In addition, the STC units encourage the use of cooperative learning to help students develop the valuable skill of working together.

In the extensive research and development process used with all STC units, scientists and educators, including experienced elementary school teachers, act as consultants to teacher-developers, who research, trial teach, and write the units. The process begins with the developer researching the unit's content and pedagogy. Then, before writing the unit, the developer trial teaches lessons in public school classrooms in the metropolitan Washington, D.C., area. Once a unit is written, the NSRC evaluates its effectiveness with children by field-testing it nationally in ethnically diverse urban, rural, and suburban public schools. At the field-testing stage, the assessment sections in each unit are also evaluated by the Program Evaluation and Research Group of Lesley College, located in Cambridge, Mass. The final editions of the units reflect the incorporation of teacher and student field-test feedback and of comments on accuracy and soundness from the leading scientists and science educators who serve on the STC Advisory Panel.

The STC project would not have been possible without the generous support of numerous federal agencies, private foundations, and corporations. Supporters include the National Science Foundation, the Smithsonian Institution, the U.S. Department of Defense, the U.S. Department of Education, the John D. and Catherine T. MacArthur Foundation, the Dow Chemical Company Foundation, the Amoco Foundation, Inc., E. I. du Pont de Nemours & Company, the Hewlett-Packard Company, and the Smithsonian Institution Educational Outreach Fund.

Acknowledgments

Motion and Design was researched, developed, and written by Carol O'Donnell, edited by Judith Grumstrup-Scott, and illustrated by Max-Karl Winkler. Lynn Miller wrote the Student Activity Book. Cynthia Allen assisted with the final editorial and production work. The field-test version of the unit was developed and written by O'Donnell and Ed Lee, research associate. Other NSRC staff who contributed to the development and production of this unit include Charles N. Hardy, NSRC deputy director for information dissemination, materials development, and publications (1995–96); Joyce Lowry Weiskopf, STC project director (1992–95); Dean Trackman, publications director; Heidi M. Kupke, publications technology specialist; Dorothy Sawicki, editor/writer; and Matthew Smith, editorial assistant. The unit was evaluated by Sabra Lee, senior research associate, Program Evaluation and Research Group, Lesley College. *Motion and Design* was trial taught during the summer program at Patrick Henry Elementary School, Arlington Public Schools, Arlington, Virginia.

The educational and technical review of *Motion and Design* was conducted by:

John Layman, Professor of Physics and Curriculum and Instruction, Science Teaching Center, University of Maryland, College Park, MD

Robert Meyer, Associate Professor, School of Industry and Technology, University of Wisconsin-Stout, Menomonie, WI

Charles J. Pitts, Electrical Engineer, Science Application International Corporation, McLean, VA

Charles Vela, Lead Engineer, Mitre Corporation, McLean, VA

The NSRC would like to thank the following individuals and school systems for their assistance with the national field-testing of the unit:

Highline School District, Burien, WA
Coordinator: Judi Backman, Math/Science Coordinator
Margaret Haney, Teacher, Valley View Elementary School, SeaTac, WA
Kent Horton, Teacher, Southern Heights Elementary School, Seattle, WA
Kathy McGregor, Teacher, Madrona Elementary School, SeaTac, WA

Mesa Public Schools, Mesa, AZ
Coordinator: Jean Hamlin, Science/Social Science Specialist
Sheryl Allen, Teacher, Hawthorne Elementary School
Warren Baker, Teacher, Stevenson Elementary School
Lynn Dillon, Teacher, Hermosa Vista Elementary

Montgomery County Public Schools, Rockville, MD
Coordinator: William McDonald, Coordinator of Elementary Science
Jerry Bush, Teacher, Clearspring Elementary School, Damascus, MD
Mary Jo Eagen, Teacher, Stedwick Elementary School, Gaithersburg, MD
Joann Kress, Teacher, Lake Seneca Elementary School, Germantown, MD

Spotsylvania County Schools, Spotsylvania, VA
Coordinator: Sandra Critchfield, Associate Director of Instructional Development
Jan Westmoreland, Teacher, Smith Station Elementary School

Sheboygan Area School District, Sheboygan, WI
Coordinator: Jerry Doyle, Coordinator of Science and Mathematics
Cindy Conrad, Teacher, Longfellow Elementary School
Ron Halverson, Teacher, Jackson Elementary School
Doris Way, Teacher, Wilson Elementary School

The NSRC would also like to thank the following individuals for their contributions to the unit:

Peter P. Afflerbach, Professor, National Reading Research Center, University of Maryland, College Park, MD

David Burgevin, Production Control Officer, Office of Imaging, Printing, and Photographic Services, Smithsonian Institution, Washington, DC

Bob Ellis, Teacher, Summer Science Program, Patrick Henry Elementary School, Arlington Public Schools, Arlington, VA

Michael Grinder and Cintia Johnson, Co-Principals, Summer Program, Patrick Henry Elementary School, Arlington Public Schools, Arlington, VA

Eric Long, Photographer, Office of Imaging, Printing, and Photographic Services, Smithsonian Institution, Washington, DC

Shirley Muldowney, Race Car Driver, Armada, MI

Jeff Tinsley, Chief, Special Assignments/Photography Branch, Office of Imaging, Printing, and Photographic Services, Smithsonian Institution, Washington, DC

Fred Wells, Principal, Smith Station Elementary School, Spotsylvania County Schools, Fredericksburg, VA

STC Advisory Panel

Peter P. Afflerbach, Professor, National Reading Research Center, University of Maryland, College Park, MD

David Babcock, Director, Board of Cooperative Educational Services, Second Supervisory District, Monroe-Orleans Counties, Spencerport, NY

Judi Backman, Math/Science Coordinator, Highline Public Schools, Seattle, WA

Albert V. Baez, President, Vivamos Mejor/USA, Greenbrae, CA

Andrew R. Barron, Professor of Chemistry and Material Science, Department of Chemistry, Rice University, Houston, TX

DeAnna Banks Beane, Project Director, YouthALIVE, Association of Science-Technology Centers, Washington, DC

Audrey Champagne, Professor of Chemistry and Education, and Chair, Educational Theory and Practice, School of Education, State University of New York at Albany, Albany, NY

Sally Crissman, Faculty Member, Lower School, Shady Hill School, Cambridge, MA

Gregory Crosby, National Program Leader, U.S. Department of Agriculture Extension Service/4-H, Washington, DC

JoAnn E. DeMaria, Teacher, Hutchison Elementary School, Herndon, VA

Hubert M. Dyasi, Director, The Workshop Center, City College School of Education (The City University of New York), New York, NY

Timothy H. Goldsmith, Professor of Biology, Yale University, New Haven, CT

Patricia Jacobberger Jellison, Geologist, National Air and Space Museum, Smithsonian Institution, Washington, DC

Patricia Lauber, Author, Weston, CT

John Layman, Professor of Education and Physics, University of Maryland, College Park, MD

Sally Love, Museum Specialist, National Museum of Natural History, Smithsonian Institution, Washington, DC

Phyllis R. Marcuccio, Associate Executive Director for Publications, National Science Teachers Association, Arlington, VA

Lynn Margulis, Professor of Biology, Department of Botany, University of Massachusetts, Amherst, MA

Margo A. Mastropieri, Co-Director, Mainstreaming Handicapped Students in Science Project, Purdue University, West Lafayette, IN

Richard McQueen, Teacher/Learning Manager, Alpha High School, Gresham, OR

Alan Mehler, Professor, Department of Biochemistry and Molecular Science, College of Medicine, Howard University, Washington, DC

Philip Morrison, Professor of Physics Emeritus, Massachusetts Institute of Technology, Cambridge, MA

Phylis Morrison, Educational Consultant, Cambridge, MA

Fran Nankin, Editor, SuperScience Red, Scholastic, New York, NY

Harold Pratt, Senior Program Officer, Development of National Science Education Standards Project, National Academy of Sciences, Washington, DC

Wayne E. Ransom, Program Director, Informal Science Education Program, National Science Foundation, Washington, DC

David Reuther, Editor-in-Chief and Senior Vice President, William Morrow Books, New York, NY

Robert Ridky, Professor, Department of Geology, University of Maryland, College Park, MD

F. James Rutherford, Chief Education Officer and Director, Project 2061, American Association for the Advancement of Science, Washington, DC

David Savage, Assistant Principal, Rolling Terrace Elementary School, Montgomery County Public Schools, Rockville, MD

Thomas E. Scruggs, Co-Director, Mainstreaming Handicapped Students in Science Project, Purdue University, West Lafayette, IN

Larry Small, Science/Health Coordinator, Schaumburg School District 54, Schaumburg, IL

Michelle Smith, Publications Director, Office of Elementary and Secondary Education, Smithsonian Institution, Washington, DC

Susan Sprague, Director of Science and Social Studies, Mesa Public Schools, Mesa, AZ

Arthur Sussman, Director, Far West Regional Consortium for Science and Mathematics, Far West Laboratory, San Francisco, CA

Emma Walton, Program Director, Presidential Awards, National Science Foundation, Washington, DC, and Past President, National Science Supervisors Association

Paul H. Williams, Director, Center for Biology Education, and Professor, Department of Plant Pathology, University of Wisconsin, Madison, WI

National Science Resources Center

Douglas Lapp, Executive Director
Sally Goetz Shuler, Deputy Director for Development, External Relations, and Outreach
R. Gail Thomas, Administrative Officer
Gail Greenberg, Executive Administrative Assistant
Dottie Smith, Administrative Assistant

Publications
Dean Trackman, Director
Marilyn Fenichel, Managing Editor, STC Discovery Deck
Linda Harteker, Writer/Editor
Lynn Miller, Writer/Editor
Dorothy Sawicki, Writer/Editor
Max-Karl Winkler, Illustrator
Heidi M. Kupke, Publications Technology Specialist
Matthew Smith, Editorial Assistant
Laura Akgulian, Writer/Editor Consultant
Cynthia Allen, Writer/Editor Consultant
Judith Gıumstrup-Scott, Writer/Editor Consultant
Lois Sloan, Illustrator Consultant

Science and Technology for Children Project
Patricia K. Freitag, Director
Judith White, Program Officer, STC Discovery Deck
Wendy Binder, Research Associate
Christopher Lyon, Research Associate
Carol O'Donnell, Research Associate
Lisa Bevell, Program Assistant
Amanda Revere, Program Aide

Outreach
Leslie J. Benton, Program Officer, Technical Assistance
Julie Clyman Lee, Program Associate

Information Dissemination
Evelyn M. Ernst, Director
Rita C. Warpeha, Resource/Database Specialist
Barbara K. Johnson, Research Associate
Sarah Lanning, Program Assistant

The above individuals were members of the NSRC staff in 1996.

Contents

	Foreword	iii
	Acknowledgments	v
	Goals for *Motion and Design*	2
	Unit Overview and Materials List	3
	Teaching *Motion and Design*	6
Lesson 1	Designing Vehicles: Getting Started	19
Lesson 2	Using Drawings to Record and Build	31
Lesson 3	Pulling a Vehicle: Looking at Force	41
Lesson 4	Testing the Motion of Vehicles Carrying a Load	51
Lesson 5	Designing Vehicles to Meet Requirements	63
Lesson 6	Evaluating Vehicle Design: Looking at Rubber Band Energy	73
Lesson 7	Testing the Effects of Rubber Band Energy	81
Lesson 8	Evaluating Vehicle Design: Looking at Friction	89
Lesson 9	Designing and Building a Vehicle with a Sail	97
Lesson 10	Testing the Effects of Air Resistance on a Vehicle's Motion	107
Lesson 11	Building a Propeller-Driven Vehicle	117
Lesson 12	Analyzing the Motion and Design of a Propeller-Driven Vehicle	125
Lesson 13	Looking at Cost	133
Lesson 14	Planning Our Final Design Challenge	141
Lesson 15	Refining Our Design	155
Lesson 16	Presenting Our Final Design Challenge	161
	Post-Unit Assessment	169
	Additional Assessments	173
	Bibliography: Resources for Teachers and Students	187

Goals for *Motion and Design*

This unit provides students an opportunity to explore the physics of motion and to apply those concepts to technological design. From their experiences, students are introduced to the following concepts, skills, and attitudes.

Concepts

- A force is any push or pull on an object. An unbalanced force is needed to make a resting object move, to bring a moving object to rest, or to change the direction of a moving object.
- A force can change the speed of an object. Greater forces can change the speed of an object faster than smaller forces.
- Friction is a force that occurs when two surfaces rub together. Friction opposes motion.
- If the same force is applied to a lighter vehicle and a heavier vehicle, the speed of the lighter vehicle will change more than the speed of the heavier vehicle.
- Energy can be stored in a rubber band and released to turn an axle or spin a propeller to make a vehicle move.
- A spinning propeller exerts a force that pushes air back and moves a vehicle forward.
- Friction must be considered when a vehicle is being designed.
- Air resistance is a force that can slow the speed of a moving vehicle.
- Design requirements specify how a vehicle or other product must perform.
- Cost is often an important consideration in designing a product.
- Engineers develop, modify, and improve designs to meet specific requirements.

Skills

- Designing, building, testing, and modifying vehicles to meet design requirements.
- Building vehicles from technical two- and three-view drawings.
- Recording vehicle designs through drawing.
- Observing how an object moves and describing its motion and changes in motion.
- Measuring the time it takes a vehicle to move a given distance.
- Collecting and recording data and analyzing it to determine representative values.
- Predicting the effect of an applied force on how a vehicle moves.
- Recording and comparing distances a vehicle travels under various conditions.
- Designing a vehicle that is propelled by stored energy.
- Solving design problems using previously collected data.
- Communicating results of an investigation through record sheets, written observations, drawings, and class discussions.

Attitudes

- Recognizing the role that technological design plays in daily problem solving.
- Appreciating how science can be used to solve practical problems.
- Recognizing the importance of repeating trials to gain valid test results.
- Valuing the application of test results to future investigations.

Unit Overview and Materials List

A toddler pushes a plastic car across the floor. A young boy struggles to pull a wagon loaded with wooden blocks. A girl notices that her bicycle wheel rubs on the fender, making the bike difficult to ride. From an early age, children experience the principles of motion when they play with wheeled toys or use vehicles for recreation.

Children are also natural designers and builders. They play with whatever materials are at hand and experiment freely to try out their ideas. Children who have access to building sets learn to manipulate the parts, make changes to an object they have built, or add interesting features to it.

Motion and Design combines these two interests of young children. It enables students to analyze the motion of vehicles they have built, investigate how forces affect a vehicle's motion, and design vehicles that are propelled by stored energy.

Lesson 1 is designed to reveal to the students, and those working with them, what they already know and what questions they have about motion and design. After becoming familiar with a building set, students design and construct a simple vehicle. In Lesson 2, students make a drawing to record the vehicle they designed and built in Lesson 1 and then build a standard vehicle from a technical drawing. Students' work in Lessons 1 and 2 serves as a pre-unit assessment that is matched to corresponding assessment activities at the end of the unit.

In Lesson 3, students use the standard vehicle they built in Lesson 2 to investigate how a vehicle moves when acted on by various forces. Students create a system of falling weights to pull the vehicle. By observing how the vehicle moves when a weighted string pulls it, they can investigate how a force can change a vehicle's motion. In Lesson 4, students modify the vehicle so that it can carry a load and then investigate how different loads affect the way the vehicle responds to a force. Students measure the time it takes the vehicle to move a distance and plot the results. These two lessons set the stage for a design challenge in Lesson 5, an embedded assessment in which students must build a vehicle that moves a specified distance in a specified time. Students present their results to the class and discuss the strategies they used to meet the challenge.

In Lessons 6 through 12, students investigate self-propelled vehicles. In Lesson 6, they are challenged to move their standard vehicle with the energy stored in a twisted rubber band. Students then freely investigate what happens when they attach the rubber band to the vehicle in various ways. In Lesson 7, students perform a controlled investigation in which they determine how the number of times they wind the rubber band around the axle affects the distance the vehicle moves. This activity introduces the concept of stored energy and helps students understand that the more energy stored in the twisted rubber band, the greater the change in the vehicle's motion.

In Lesson 8, students evaluate the design of their axle-driven vehicles, looking specifically at friction and design features that may enhance or oppose the vehicles' motion. Through discussion of how parts of the vehicle can rub together, students grasp the idea that friction affects vehicle performance and must be considered during design. In Lessons 9 and 10, students extend their knowledge of friction as they design vehicles with a sail and test the effects of "air friction," or air resistance, on the motion of their vehicles.

In Lessons 11 and 12, students apply what they have learned about the physics of motion and the process of design to the building and testing of a vehicle driven by a propeller. Using a three-view technical drawing in Lesson 11, students build a propeller-driven vehicle. By modifying independent design features of the propeller-driven vehicle in Lesson 12 and determining the effects of each design modification on the vehicle's motion, they engage in a more challenging design problem.

Lesson 13 introduces students to another design requirement—cost. Given the value of each building piece, students determine the total cost of their propeller-driven vehicles and then redesign them to reduce this amount. After retesting their vehicles to ensure they still move and making further modifications if necessary, students determine the final reduced cost of their vehicles.

Lessons 14 through 16, a second embedded assessment, enable students to apply what they have learned throughout the unit to a final design challenge. In Lesson 14, students work in cooperative teams of six and choose one of several design challenges. In a planning session, they decide on the vehicle design, system for moving the vehicle, cost, and method of testing. Then they sketch their proposed vehicle. In Lesson 15, each team builds, tests, refines, and retests its vehicle, making certain it is within the proposed budget. Teams then present their final design solutions in Lesson 16 and conclude with a reflective writing activity.

Following Lesson 16 is a post-unit assessment that is matched to the pre-unit assessment in Lesson 1. The additional assessments provide further questions and challenges for evaluating students' progress, including the examination of real-world vehicles and the development of portfolios in which students organize and display a selection of their work from the unit.

This is a rich unit for students. Just as engineers do, students test their vehicle designs and repeatedly evaluate and refine them until the designs meet specifications. They apply physics concepts to solve practical problems. Their introduction to technical drawing improves their record-keeping skills and extends their visual perception. As a class, students share in the creativity of solving problems, testing ideas, and presenting results. Finally, students reflect on their work throughout the unit and grasp how they can apply these problem-solving skills and concepts in their own world.

Materials List

Below is a list of the materials needed for the *Motion and Design* unit. Please note that the metric and English equivalents in this unit are approximate.

- 1 *Motion and Design* Teacher's Guide
- 15 *Motion and Design* Student Activity Books
- 1 STC set of K'NEX® building pieces
- 11 buckets with lids
- 10 measuring tapes, 100 cm (39 in)
- 10 sets of colored pencils
- 300 sheets of three-hole, ¼-in (10-mm) graph paper with light blue lines, 21.5 × 28 cm (8½ × 11 in)
- 1 package of assorted colored markers
- 1 fine-point, permanent black marker
- 10 circle templates
- 1 spool of light string
- 1 box of jumbo paper clips
- 30 large metal washers
- 220 small metal washers
- 10 small plastic cups, 30 ml (1 oz)
- 10 large bookends with nonslip base, 23h × 15w × 20d cm (9h × 6w × 8d in), about 0.5 kg (1 lb)
- 10 timers
- 20 blocks of wood, 5 × 8 × 9 cm (2 × 3 × 3½ in)
- 60 self-stick red dots, 2 cm (¾ in) diameter
- 60 self-stick blue dots, 2 cm (¾ in) diameter
- 30 self-stick green dots, 2 cm (¾ in) diameter
- 100 small rubber bands, No. 16
- 40 large rubber bands, No. 64
  Adding machine tape, at least 80 m (262½ ft)
- 10 pieces of cardboard, 21.5 × 28 cm (8½ × 11 in)
- 30 pairs of safety goggles
- 25 brass eyelets
- 11 two-bladed propellers, with 18-cm (7-in) span
- 11 screw hooks, 0.3 cm (⅛ in) diameter
- *30 pencils with erasers
- *600 sheets of lined, loose-leaf paper, 21.5 × 28 cm (8½ × 11 in)
- *30 science notebooks (folders or binders)
- * Newsprint
- *10 metric rulers
- *2 rolls of masking tape
- *2 Post-it® notepads, 7.6 × 12.7 cm (3 × 5 in)
- *10 scissors
- *2 single-hole punches (optional)
- *10 calculators (optional)
- *2 small electric fans (optional)
- * Books (for elevating runway)
- * Trade books about load-bearing vehicles
- **10 strips of Masonite™, 38 × 122 × 0.6 cm (15 × 48 × ¼ in), or foamboard, 38 × 122 × 0.5 cm (15 × 48 × 3⁄16 in)

*Note: These items are not included in the kit. They are available in most schools or can be brought from home.

**Note: Masonite™ or foamboard is not included in the kit because it is needed only by schools without access to long tables. Masonite can be purchased at a hardware store and cut to size. Foamboard can be purchased at an art or office supply store, or the strips for this unit can be ordered from Carolina Biological Supply Company.

Teaching *Motion and Design*

The following information on unit structure, teaching strategies, materials, and assessment will help you give students the guidance they need to make the most of their hands-on experiences with this unit.

Unit Structure

Organization of Lessons in the Teacher's Guide: Each lesson in the *Motion and Design* Teacher's Guide provides you with a brief overview, lesson objectives, key background information, a materials list, advance preparation instructions, step-by-step procedures, and helpful management tips. Many of the lessons include recommended guidelines for assessment. Lessons also frequently indicate opportunities for curriculum integration. Look for the following icons that highlight extension ideas:

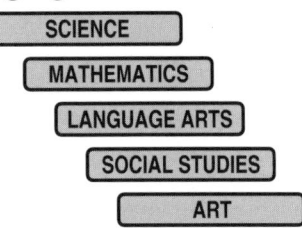

Please note that all record sheets, blackline masters, student instructions, and reading selections may be copied and used in conjunction with the teaching of this unit.

Student Activity Book: The *Motion and Design* Student Activity Book accompanies the Teacher's Guide. Written specifically for students, this activity book contains simple instructions and illustrations to enable students to conduct the activities in this unit. The Student Activity Book will help students follow along with you as you guide each lesson. It will also provide guidance for students who may miss a lesson or for those who do not immediately grasp certain activities or concepts. In addition to previewing each lesson in the Teacher's Guide, you may find it helpful to preview the accompanying lesson in the Student Activity Book.

The lessons in the Student Activity Book are divided into the following sections, paralleling the Teacher's Guide:

- **Think and Wonder** sketches for students a general picture of the ideas and activities of the lesson described in the Overview and Objectives of the Teacher's Guide.

- **Materials** lists the materials students and their partners or teammates will be using.

- **Find Out for Yourself** flows in tandem with the steps in the **Procedure** and **Final Activities** sections of the Teacher's Guide and briefly and simply walks students through the lesson's activities.

- **Ideas to Explore,** which frequently echoes the Extensions section in the Teacher's Guide, gives students additional activities to try out or ideas to think about.

Teaching Strategies

Classroom Discussion: Class discussions, effectively led by the teacher, are important vehicles for science learning. Research shows that the way questions are asked, as well as the time allowed for responses, can contribute to the quality of the discussion.

When you ask questions, think about what you want to achieve in the ensuing discussion. For example, open-ended questions, for which there is no single right answer, will encourage students to give creative and thoughtful answers. You can use other types of questions to encourage students to see specific relationships and contrasts or to help them summarize and draw conclusions. It is good practice to mix these questions. It also is good practice always to give students "wait time" before expecting them to answer; this will encourage broader participation and more thoughtful answers. You will want to monitor responses, looking for additional situations that invite students to formulate hypotheses, make generalizations, and explain how they arrived at a conclusion.

Brainstorming: Brainstorming is a whole-class exercise in which students contribute their thoughts about a particular idea or problem. When used to introduce a new science topic, it can be a stimulating and productive exercise. It also is a useful and efficient way for the teacher to find out what students know and think about a topic. As students learn the rules for brainstorming, they will become increasingly adept in their participation.

To begin a brainstorming session, define for students the topics about which they will share ideas. Explain the following rules to students:

- Accept all ideas without judgment.
- Do not criticize or make unnecessary comments about the contributions of others.
- Try to connect your ideas to the ideas of others.

Webbing: Webbing enables you to record ideas in a graphic display with the main subject at the center, or nucleus, of the web. The advantage of webbing is that it identifies relationships between related ideas and the nucleus. Webbing helps students recognize what they already know about a subject and invites them to make as many associations as they can about it. "Concept mapping" and "clustering" are other names for webbing. Figure T-1 illustrates a web on vehicles that students create during a brainstorming session in the *Motion and Design* unit.

Venn Diagrams: Venn diagrams are useful tools for recording information to be compared. Venn diagrams use two or more intersecting circles to represent different sets of information. Information that relates to one idea is written inside one of the circles. Information about a similar yet different idea is written inside another circle. Information common to both ideas is written in the area of intersection. Although it is not suggested to use Venn diagrams at any one point in the unit, they can be a powerful tool for comparing results or making comparative observations.

Cooperative Learning Groups: One of the best ways to teach hands-on science is to arrange students in small groups. Materials and procedures for most *Motion and Design* activities are based on groups of three. There are several advantages to this organization. It provides a small forum in which students can express their ideas and get feedback. It also offers students a chance to learn from each other by sharing ideas, discoveries, and skills. With coaching, students can develop interpersonal skills that will serve them

Figure T-1

Webbing ideas

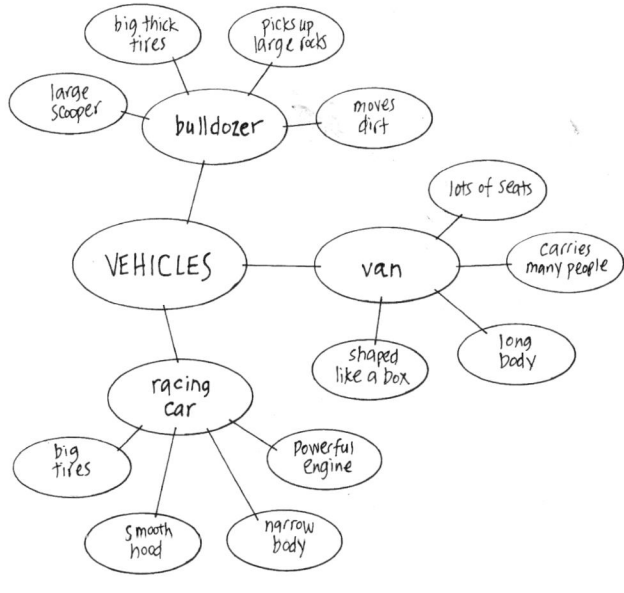

well in all aspects of life. Encourage groups to allow each member to handle and manipulate the building pieces and vehicles in each lesson. Help students assign roles to each member, such as mathematician, artist, builder, or technical writer, and assign tasks within each investigation. This way, each member of the group is assured time to contribute his or her ideas to the final product.

As students work, they will often find it productive to talk about what they are doing, resulting in a steady hum of conversation. If you or others in the school are accustomed to a quiet room, this busy atmosphere may require some adjustment.

Learning Centers: You can give supplemental science materials a permanent home in the classroom in a spot designated as the learning center. Students can use the center in a number of ways: as an "on your own" project center, as an observation post, as a trade book reading nook, or simply as a place to spend unscheduled time when assignments are done. To keep interest in the center high, change the learning center or add to it often. Here are a few suggestions of items to include:

- Science trade books about different types of vehicles, motion, design, and inventions and how things work (see Bibliography for suggested titles).

- The class bucket of building pieces for students to design and build on their own.
- Audiovisual materials on related subjects.
- Items contributed by students for sharing.
- Additional activities for hands-on investigation.

Materials

Safety: This unit does not contain anything highly toxic, but common sense dictates that nothing be put in the mouth. It is good practice to tell your students that, in science class, materials are never tasted. The building set in this unit contains small pieces that should not be placed in the mouth. Students should be careful when removing the small pieces, which can pop off and fly through the air. Instruct them to wear safety goggles when handling the rubber bands and propellers.

Organization of Materials: To help ensure an orderly progression through the unit, you will need to establish a system for storing and distributing materials. Being prepared is the key to success. Here are a few suggestions:

- Read through the **Materials List** on pg. 5. Begin to collect the items you will need that are not provided in the kit.

- Organize your students so they are involved in distributing and returning materials. If you already have cooperative groups established, delegate the responsibility to one member of each group.

- Organize a distribution center and instruct students to pick up and return supplies to that area. A cafeteria-style approach works especially well when there are large numbers of items to distribute.

- Look at each lesson ahead of time. Some have specific suggestions for handling materials needed that day.

- Management tips are provided throughout the unit. Look for this icon:

Assessment

Philosophy: In the Science and Technology for Children program, assessment is an ongoing, integral part of instruction. Because assessment emerges naturally from the activities in the lessons, students are assessed in the same manner in which they are taught. They may, for example, perform experiments, record their observations, or make oral presentations. Such assessments permit the examination of processes as well as of products, emphasizing what students know and can do.

The learning goals in STC units include a number of different science concepts, skills, and attitudes. Therefore, a number of different strategies are provided to help you assess and document your students' progress toward the goals (see Figure T-2). These strategies also will help you report to parents and appraise your own teaching. In addition, the assessments will enable your students to view their own progress, reflect on their learning, and formulate further questions for investigation and research.

Figure T-2 summarizes the goals and assessment strategies for this unit. The left-hand column lists the individual goals for the *Motion and Design* unit and the lessons in which they are addressed. The right-hand column identifies lessons containing assessment sections to which you can turn for specific assessment strategies. These strategies are summarized as bulleted items.

Assessment Strategies: The assessment strategies in STC units fall into three categories: matched pre- and post-unit assessments, embedded assessments, and additional assessments.

The first lesson of each STC unit is a *pre-unit assessment* designed to give you information about what the entire class and individual students already know about the unit's topic and what they want to find out. It often includes a brainstorming session during which students share their thoughts about the topic through exploring one or two basic questions. In the *post-unit assessment* following the final lesson, the class revisits the pre-unit assessment questions, giving you two sets of comparable data that indicate students' growth in knowledge and skills (see Figure T-3).

Throughout a unit, assessments are incorporated, or embedded, into lessons. These *embedded assessments* are activities that occur naturally within the context of both the individual lesson and the unit as a whole; they are often indistinguishable from instructional activities. By providing structured activities and guidelines for assessing students' progress and thinking, embedded assessments contribute to an ongoing, detailed profile of growth. In *Motion and Design*, Lesson 5 and Lessons 14 through 16 serve as embedded assessments that challenge students to synthesize and apply concepts or skills from the unit.

continued on pg. 14

Figure T-2

Motion and Design: **Goals and Assessment Strategies**

Concepts	
Goals	**Assessment Strategies**
A force is any push or pull on an object. An unbalanced force is needed to make a resting object move, to bring a moving object to rest, or to change the direction of a moving object. Lessons 1, 3–8, 10–12, 14–16	Lessons 1, 5, 9, 12, 14, 16, and Additional Assessments 1 and 2 • Pre- and post-unit assessments • Class discussions • Student investigations • Record sheets • Oral presentations • Student self-assessment
A force can change the speed of an object. Greater forces can change the speed of an object faster than smaller forces. Lessons 1, 3, 5, 7, 12, 14–16	Lessons 1, 5, 9, 12, 14, 16, and Additional Assessments 1 and 2 • Pre- and post-unit assessments • Class discussions and lists • Student investigations • Record sheets • Oral presentations • Teacher observations • Student self-assessment
Friction is a force that occurs when two surfaces rub together. Friction opposes motion. Lessons 3, 7–10, 12, 14–16	Lessons 1, 9, 12, 14, 16, and Additional Assessments 1, 2, and 3 • Pre- and post-unit assessments • Class discussions and lists • Student investigations • Record sheets • Oral presentations • Teacher observations • Building vehicles • Student self-assessment
If the same force is applied to a lighter vehicle and a heavier vehicle, the speed of the lighter vehicle will change more than the speed of the heavier vehicle. Lessons 4, 5, 10, 12, 14–16	Lessons 5, 9, 14, 16, and Additional Assessments 1 and 2 • Class discussions and lists • Student investigations • Record sheets • Oral presentations • Teacher observations • Student self-assessment
Energy can be stored in a rubber band and released to turn an axle or spin a propeller to make a vehicle move. Lessons 6–16	Lessons 9, 12, 14, 16, and Additional Assessments 1 and 2 • Post-unit assessments • Class discussions and lists • Student investigations • Record sheets • Oral presentations • Teacher observations • Building vehicles • Student self-assessment
A spinning propeller exerts a force that pushes air back and moves a vehicle forward. Lessons 11–16	Lessons 12, 14, 16, and Additional Assessments 1, 2, and 3 • Post-unit assessments • Class discussions and lists • Student investigations • Record sheets • Oral presentations • Teacher observations • Building vehicles • Student self-assessment

Figure T-2: *Motion and Design:* Goals and Assessment Strategies, Concepts *(continued)*

Goals	Assessment Strategies
Friction must be considered when a vehicle is being designed. 　Lessons 1, 5, 8–12, 14–16	Lessons 1, 9, 12, 14, 16, and Additional Assessments 1, 2, 3, and 4 　▪ Pre- and post-unit assessments 　▪ Class discussions and lists 　▪ Student investigations 　▪ Record sheets 　▪ Student drawings 　▪ Oral presentations 　▪ Teacher observations 　▪ Building vehicles 　▪ Student self-assessment
Air resistance is a force that can slow the speed of a moving vehicle. 　Lesson 9, 10, 14–16	Lessons 9, 12, 14, 16, and Additional Assessments 1, 2, 3, and 4 　▪ Pre- and post-unit assessments 　▪ Class discussions and lists 　▪ Student investigations 　▪ Record sheets 　▪ Student drawings 　▪ Oral presentations 　▪ Teacher observations 　▪ Building vehicles 　▪ Student self-assessment
Design requirements specify how a vehicle or other product must perform. 　Lessons 5, 6, 9, 14–16	Lessons 1, 5, 14, 16, and Additional Assessments 2 and 3 　▪ Pre- and post-unit assessments 　▪ Class discussions and lists 　▪ Student investigations 　▪ Record sheets 　▪ Oral presentations 　▪ Teacher observations 　▪ Building vehicles
Cost is often an important consideration in designing a product. 　Lessons 13–16	Lessons 14, 16, and Additional Assessment 3 　▪ Class discussions and lists 　▪ Record sheets 　▪ Oral presentations 　▪ Building vehicles
Engineers develop, modify, and improve designs to meet specific requirements. 　Lessons 1, 2, 5, 8, 9, 11–16	Lessons 1, 2, 5, 9, 12, 14, 16, and Additional Assessments 1, 2, and 3 　▪ Pre- and post-unit assessments 　▪ Class discussions and lists 　▪ Student investigations 　▪ Record sheets 　▪ Student drawings 　▪ Oral presentations 　▪ Teacher observations 　▪ Building vehicles 　▪ Student self-assessment

Skills	
Goals	**Assessment Strategies**
Designing, building, testing, and modifying vehicles to meet design requirements. Lessons 1, 2, 5, 8, 9, 11–16	Lessons 1, 2, 5, 9, 12, 14, 16, and Additional Assessments 1, 2, and 3 - Pre- and post-unit assessments - Class discussions and lists - Student investigations - Record sheets - Student drawings - Oral presentations - Teacher observations - Building vehicles - Student self-assessment
Building vehicles from technical two- and three-view drawings. Lessons 2, 11, 14–16	Lessons 2, 12, 14, 16 - Student drawings - Teacher observations - Building vehicles
Recording vehicle designs through drawing Lessons 2, 5, 9, 14–16	Lessons 2, 5, 9, 12, 14, 16, and Additional Assessment 4 - Record sheets - Student drawings - Teacher observations
Observing how an object moves and describing its motion and changes in motion. Lessons 1, 3–8, 10, 12, 13–16	Lessons 1, 5, 12, 14, 16, and Additional Assessments 2 and 3 - Pre- and post-unit assessments - Class discussions and lists - Student investigations - Record sheets - Oral presentations - Teacher observations
Measuring the time it takes a vehicle to move a given distance. Lessons 1, 4, 5, 14–16	Lessons 1, 5, 14, 16, and Additional Assessment 2 - Pre- and post-unit assessments - Student investigations - Record sheets - Oral presentations - Teacher observations
Collecting and recording data and analyzing it to determine representative values. Lessons 4, 5, 7, 10, 14–16	Lessons 1, 5, 14, 16, and Additional Assessment 2 - Pre- and post-unit assessments - Student investigations - Record sheets - Oral presentations - Teacher observations
Predicting the effect of an applied force on how a vehicle moves. Lessons 1, 3–5, 7–10, 12, 14–16	Lessons 1, 5, 12, 14, 16, and Additional Assessments 1 and 2 - Pre- and post-unit assessments - Class discussions and lists - Student investigations - Record sheets - Oral presentations
Recording and comparing distances a vehicle travels under various conditions. Lessons 1, 7, 12, 14–16	Lessons 1, 12, 14, 16, and Additional Assessment 2 - Pre- and post-unit assessments - Class discussions and lists - Student investigations - Record sheets - Oral presentations

Figure T-2: Motion and Design: Goals and Assessment Strategies, Skills *(continued)*

Goals	Assessment Strategies
Designing a vehicle that is propelled by stored energy. Lessons 6–16	Lessons 9, 12, 14, 16, and Additional Assessments 2 and 4 • Post-unit assessments • Student investigations • Record sheets • Student drawings • Oral presentations • Teacher observations • Building vehicles
Solving design problems using previously collected data. Lesson 5, 10, 14–16	Lessons 5, 9, 14, 16, and Additional Assessment 2 • Student investigations • Record sheets • Teacher observations • Building vehicles
Communicating results of an investigation through record sheets, written observations, drawings, and class discussions. Lessons 1–10, 12–16	Lessons 1, 2, 5, 9, 12, 14, 16, and Additional Assessments 2, 3, and 4 • Pre- and post-unit assessments • Class discussions and lists • Student investigations • Record sheets • Student drawings • Oral presentations • Teacher observations • Student self-assessment

Attitudes	
Goals	**Assessment Strategies**
Recognizing the role that technological design plays in daily problem solving. Lessons 1, 2, 5, 6, 8–16	Lessons 1, 2, 5, 9, 12, 14, 16, and Additional Assessments 1, 2, 3, and 4 • Pre- and post-unit assessments • Class discussions and lists • Student investigations • Record sheets • Student drawings • Oral presentations • Teacher observations • Building vehicles • Student self-assessment
Appreciating how science can be used to solve practical problems. Lessons 1, 2, 5, 6, 8–16	Lessons 1, 2, 5, 9, 12, 14, 16, and Additional Assessments 1, 2, 3, and 4 • Pre- and post-unit assessments • Class discussions and lists • Student investigations • Record sheets • Student drawings • Oral presentations • Teacher observations • Building vehicles • Student self-assessment

Attitudes *(continued)*

Goals	Assessment Strategies
Recognizing the importance of repeating trials to gain valid test results. 　Lessons 3–5, 7, 10, 14–16	Lessons 1, 5, 14, 16, and Additional Assessments 2 and 4 ▪ Pre- and post-unit assessments ▪ Class discussions and lists ▪ Student investigations ▪ Record sheets ▪ Teacher observations
Valuing the application of test results to future investigations. 　Lessons 1, 3–5, 9, 7, 10, 14–15	Lessons 1, 5, 9, 14, 16, and Additional Assessments 2 and 4 ▪ Pre- and post-unit assessments ▪ Student investigations ▪ Record sheets ▪ Teacher observations ▪ Building vehicles ▪ Student self-assessment

continued from pg. 8

Figure T-3

Sample of matched pre- and post-unit class lists

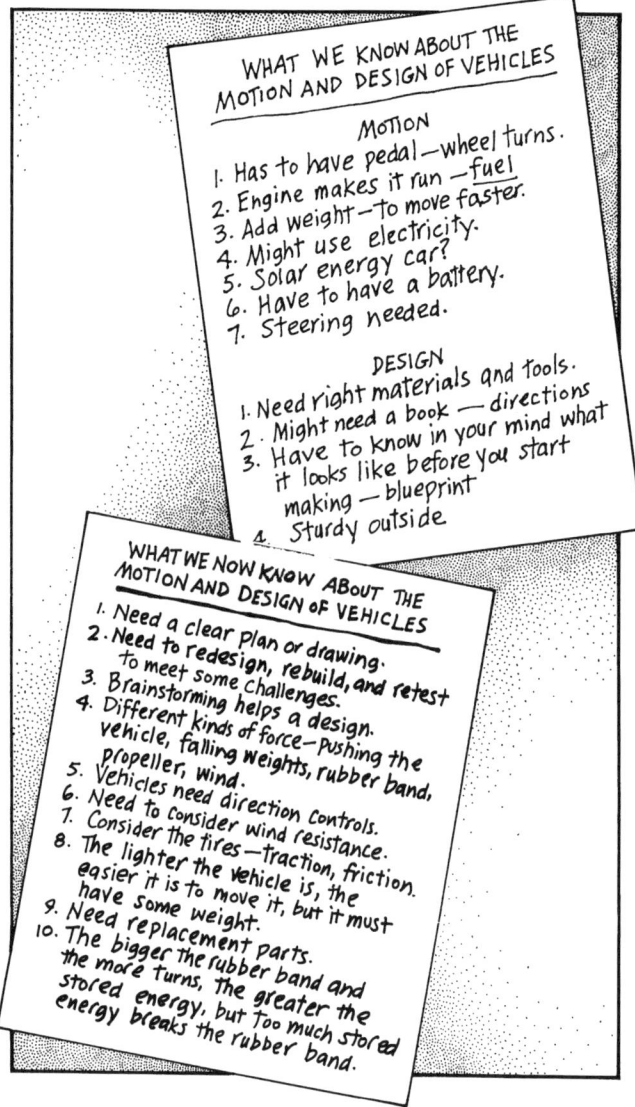

Additional assessments can be used to determine students' understanding after the unit has been completed. In these assessments, students may work with materials to solve problems, conduct experiments, or interpret and organize data. In *Motion and Design*, students also complete a self-assessment. To monitor growth, students complete the assessment in Lesson 9 and again at the end of the unit. When you are selecting additional assessments, consider using more than one. This will give students with different learning styles additional opportunities to express their knowledge and skills.

Documenting Student Performance: In STC units, assessment is based on your recorded observations, students' work products, and oral communication. All these documentation methods combine to give you a comprehensive picture of each student's growth.

Teachers' *observations and anecdotal notes* often provide the most useful information about students' understanding. Because it is important to document observations used for assessment, teachers frequently keep note cards, journals, or checklists. Many lessons include guidelines to help you focus your observations. The blackline master *Motion and Design*: Observations of Student Performance (pg. 16) provides a format you may want to use or adapt for recording observations. It includes this unit's goals for science concepts and skills.

Work products, which include both what students write and what they make, indicate students' progress toward the goals of the unit. Children produce a variety of written materials during a unit. Record sheets, which include written observations, drawings, graphs, tables, and charts, are an important part of all STC units. They provide evidence of each student's ability to collect, record, and process information. Students' science notebooks are another type of work product. Often a rich source of information for assessment, these notebook entries reveal students' thoughts, ideas, and questions over time. Drawings of students' vehicles are another type of work product in *Motion and Design*, which together with photographs, visually display how students met the design requirements. Drawings and photographs of the vehicles, selected by students and teacher, can be used to develop student portfolios at the close of the unit.

Students' written work products should be kept together in folders to document learning over the course of the unit. When students refer back to their work from previous lessons, they can reflect on their learning. In some cases, students do not write or draw well enough for their products to be used for assessment purposes, but their experiences do contribute to the development of scientific literacy.

Oral communication, what students say formally and informally in class and in individual sessions with you, is a particularly useful way to learn what students know. This unit provides your students with many opportunities to share and discuss their own ideas, observations, and opinions. Some children may be experiencing such activities for the first time. Encourage students to participate in discussions, and stress that there are no right or wrong responses.

Creating an environment in which students feel secure expressing their own ideas can stimulate rich and diverse discussions.

Individual and group presentations can give you insights about the meanings your students have assigned to procedures and concepts and about their confidence in their learning. In fact, a student's verbal description of a chart, experiment, or graph is frequently more useful for assessment than the product or results. Questions posed by other students following presentations provide yet another opportunity for you to gather information. Ongoing records of discussions and presentations should be a part of your documentation of students' learning.

Blackline Master

Motion and Design: Observations of Student Performance

STUDENT'S NAME:

Concepts	Observations
• A force is any push or pull on an object. An unbalanced force is needed to make a resting object move, to bring a moving object to rest, or to change the direction of a moving object. • A force can change the speed of an object. Greater forces can change the speed of an object faster than smaller forces. • Friction is a force that occurs when two surfaces rub together. Friction opposes motion. • If the same force is applied to a lighter vehicle and a heavier vehicle, the speed of the lighter vehicle will change more than the speed of the heavier vehicle. • Energy can be stored in a rubber band and released to turn an axle or spin a propeller to make a vehicle move. • A spinning propeller exerts a force that pushes air back and moves a vehicle forward. • Friction must be considered when a vehicle is being designed. • Air resistance is a force that can slow the speed of a moving vehicle. • Design requirements specify how a vehicle or other product must perform. • Cost is often an important consideration in designing a product. • Engineers develop, modify, and improve designs to meet specific requirements.	

Skills

- Designing, building, testing, and modifying vehicles to meet design requirements.
- Building vehicles from technical two- and three-view drawings.
- Recording vehicle designs through drawing.
- Observing how an object moves and describing its motion and changes in motion.
- Measuring the time it takes a vehicle to move a given distance.
- Collecting and recording data and analyzing it to determine representative values.
- Predicting the effect of an applied force on how a vehicle moves.
- Recording and comparing distances a vehicle travels under various conditions.
- Designing a vehicle that is propelled by stored energy.
- Solving design problems using previously collected data.
- Communicating results of an investigation through record sheets, written observations, drawings, and class discussions.

STC / *Motion and Design*

LESSON 1

Designing Vehicles: Getting Started

Overview and Objectives

This lesson introduces students to the physics of motion and the challenge of technological design. It asks them to write what they already know and what questions they have about how vehicles move and how they are designed. This lesson also provides important pre-unit assessment information about students' understanding of motion and design. Additional assessment information can be obtained when students share their understanding of the concepts of motion and design in a brainstorming activity and demonstrate their skills by designing and building a vehicle.

- Students set up their science notebooks.
- Students record and share their ideas and questions about motion and design.
- Students design and build a vehicle to meet certain requirements.

Background

About 2,000 years ago, Aristotle taught that an object can move only if it is pushed by a force and that movement stops when the force is removed. Aristotle's view was shaped by his experience with motion in the presence of friction, such as pulling a heavily loaded wagon. However, he could not explain why a ball continues to move through the air after it leaves the thrower's hand. In the sixteenth century, Galileo recognized that no force is needed to keep an object moving—only to start it, stop it, or change its direction or speed. In 1687, Isaac Newton expanded on Galileo's work and proposed three laws of motion.

Newton's first law of motion states that an object at rest remains at rest and an object in motion remains in motion in a straight line, unless acted on by a force. Newton's second law states that when a force acts on an object, the object will start to move, speed up, slow down, or change direction in direct proportion to the magnitude of the force and inversely proportional to the mass of the object. The greater the force, the greater the change of motion; the greater the mass of the object, the smaller the change of motion. And finally, Newton's third law states that if an object exerts a force on a second object, the second object exerts an equal and opposite force on the first object.

These laws serve as a foundation for the science of **dynamics,** a branch of physics that focuses on forces and their relation to motion (and to the absence of motion). In *Motion and Design*, students have the opportunity to explore some basic aspects of Newton's laws as they model the practice of engineers and design vehicles using the principles and problem-solving skills of technological design.

LESSON 1

Technology is the development and use of products, systems, or environments that solve problems and extend human capabilities. The computer, pulley, wheel, and even the pencil are results of technological innovation. These devices have made life easier. Engineers apply their knowledge of science and mathematics to the solution of practical problems. Although science and engineering are related, they have different goals. The scientist's goal is to acquire a systematic knowledge of the physical and material world, whereas the engineer's goal is to apply that knowledge to the design and creation of a product that meets a need. The product might be an object, such as a bridge or an automobile, a system, such as an improved way to recycle paper, or an environment.

Why people need a product and how they will use it help engineers determine the product's design requirements. The design requirements for an automobile, for instance, might be that it have a maximum speed of 130 km (80 miles) per hour and cost less than $20,000. Often an engineer will create a **prototype**—the original or model on which something is patterned—to test whether the final product is likely to meet the design requirements.

For example, aeronautical engineers build models of aircraft and test the airflow around them in wind tunnels. Naval architects perform similar tests with models of boats in water tanks. For such tests, engineers create requirements appropriate for the small size of the model. If the model does not satisfy these requirements, engineers search for improvements and modify the model. If a particular design continues to fail, the engineers go "back to the drawing board" and start over. This process of identifying a problem, creating a solution, evaluating the solution by testing, and then refining the design to improve performance is the essence of the process of **technological design.** According to the International Technology Education Association, "Technological design involves the application of knowledge to new situations or goals, resulting in the development of new knowledge."

Students will discover that the steps in design processes are **recursive;** in other words, at any point in the process, one can return to a previous step to make improvements. In this unit, students will go through the steps shown in the technological design process in Figure 1-1. The design is refined again and again until an optimum product is obtained. The variety of task-specific concepts, skills, and attitudes that accompany this process can be applied to many other problem-solving situations, including landscape architecture and graphic design.

Throughout the unit, students will be given several challenges, often with requirements specifying the distance a vehicle must move and the time it must

Figure 1-1

A technological design process

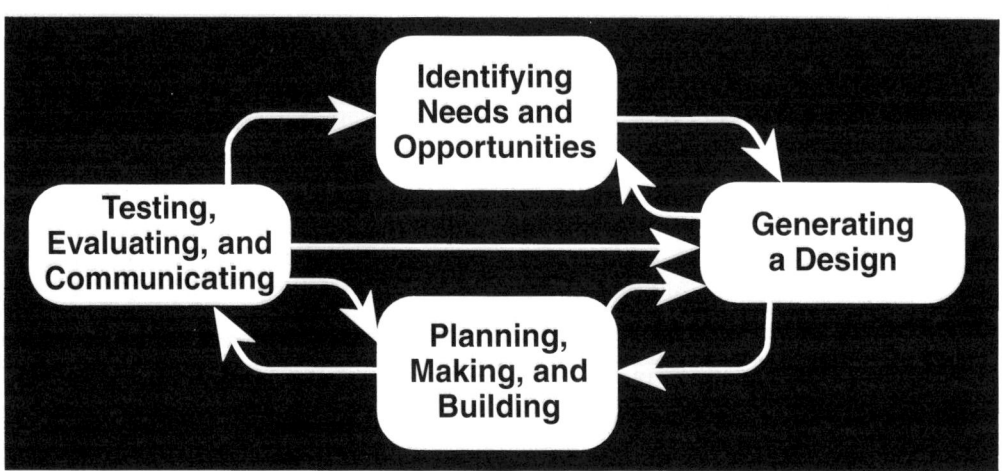

move the distance. For example, "Design a delivery truck that will carry a load of four wooden blocks a distance of 1 m in 4 seconds or less." The challenge might specify that students use a particular system (for example, "Use falling weights").

After students receive a challenge, they are given the opportunity to conduct research for their design by evaluating existing products or processes. For example, they might review trade books on trucks and vans or evaluate existing vehicle designs before designing their own vehicles to carry a load.

To complete their design challenges and explore concepts of motion, students will use a set of building pieces. These pieces connect in a variety of ways, offering great opportunity for creative design. When students first use the pieces, you may need to move about the classroom to assist them with their design problems. Encourage each student to handle the vehicle being built by the group. To ensure that each student contributes to the building process, you may wish to announce periodically that it is time to pass the vehicle to the next group member. Guide students in removing or attaching small pieces. Supply extra pieces as needed.

Although students will build at various paces, some design challenges have a time requirement. The time requirement might be: "Complete the challenge in 20 minutes or less." Remind students throughout the unit that engineers often have time requirements for their tasks. The length of time suggested for each challenge is noted in some lessons. Feel free, however, to adapt these times to suit your class.

Because students will be working in groups of three in most lessons, you may need to discuss with them the importance of cooperative problem solving. Encourage students to agree on the assignment of responsibility for particular work roles within the group. Consider the following roles:

- **Materials Manager**—picks up the group's materials from the distribution center, helps the group return materials to the center, and makes certain all materials are inventoried and in order.

- **Moderator**—keeps the group on task, makes certain each member has a chance to contribute, and helps the team work together.

- **Reporter**—communicates the group's ideas to the class and reads instructions to the group.

- **Recorder**—records information to be shared with the class and records observations on the group record sheets.

- **Investigator**—asks questions of the teacher, as needed, while the group works.

In *Motion and Design,* some other appropriate assignments within the group might be chief engineer, math engineer, artist, builder, and technical writer. Help students select their roles for this unit.

Note: The **Background** in each lesson is meant to help you prepare for the lesson and is not intended for use with students. There are many opportunities in the unit for students to discover the new ideas in the lesson for themselves through investigations, discussions, and reading selections.

Materials

For each student

- 1 science notebook
- 1 pencil with eraser
- 10 sheets of three-hole, ¼-in (10-mm) graph paper, 21.5 × 28 cm (8½ × 11 in)
- 20 sheets of loose-leaf paper, 21.5 × 28 cm (8½ × 11 in)

LESSON 1

For each group of three students
- 1 copy of **Building Pieces for Each Group** (blackline master, pg. 28)
- 1 STC set of K'NEX® building pieces
- 1 copy of **Tips on Using the Building Pieces** (blackline master, pg. 29) (optional)
- 1 bucket and lid

For the class
- 15 *Motion and Design* Student Activity Books
- 2 sheets of newsprint
- 1 black permanent marker
- 10 measuring tapes, 100 cm (39 in)
- 10 timers
- 1 Post-it® notepad, 7.6 × 12.7 cm (3 × 5 in)
  Masking tape
  Assorted colored markers
- 1 bucket
  Extra building pieces (stored in bucket)

Preparation

1. Set up a time before starting this lesson when students can freely explore the building pieces and timers.

2. You may wish to familiarize yourself with the materials by making some simple constructions. It is helpful to be thoroughly familiar with how the pieces fit together. Use the blackline master **Tips on Using the Building Pieces** (pg. 29) as a guide.

3. Decide if you want your students to use the blackline master Tips on Using the Building Pieces (pg. 29) during this lesson. If so, make one copy for each group.

4. Students use the Student Activity Books in groups of three during most of their investigations. They will use the books in groups of two when you assign reading selections. Decide when during the lesson you want to distribute the Student Activity Books.

5. Title one sheet of newsprint as follows: "What We Know about the Motion and Design of Vehicles." Date and hang the newsprint sheet.

6. Label the second sheet of newsprint "What We Want to Find Out about Motion and Design." Date the sheet and set it aside.

7. Decide how you would like to divide the class into groups of three. Keep in mind that you may want groups to remain together throughout the unit. Some teachers have found success with grouping students by gender. You can also create groups with a mix of aptitudes—for example, one member strong in math, one in art, and one in writing. Assign a letter to each group.

8. Decide what to use for the students' science notebooks. Folders with pockets and fasteners for three-hole paper work well. Students will use these notebooks to record daily observations and store their record sheets. Each student will place in the notebook 20 sheets of lined loose-leaf paper for written entries and 10 sheets of graph paper for drawings.

9. Arrange your classroom so that each group sits at a table or at three desks pushed together. Two of the desks should be the same height. This will be vital in Lessons 3 and 4.

10. For each group of three students, make one copy of the blackline master **Building Pieces for Each Group** (pg. 28). Groups should store this list in their buckets.

11. Divide the building pieces so that each group receives an identical set, as listed on the blackline master Building Pieces for Each Group. You may wish to solicit the help of student or adult volunteers for this task. Put each group's set in a plastic bucket, insert a copy of Building Pieces for Each Group in the bucket, and cover the bucket with a lid. Because students will sometimes borrow pieces from another group, you may want to ask groups to periodically use the blackline master to inventory their building pieces.

12. Place all extra building pieces in the "class" bucket. These pieces can be used by groups as needed throughout the unit.

13. Using a black permanent marker, label each bucket and lid with a group letter.

14. Arrange the materials at a distribution center, as shown in Figure 1-2. Set out the science notebooks, sheets of loose-leaf and graph paper, and buckets of building pieces. Label the materials at the distribution center with the item name and the amount needed by each group. Set the timers and measuring tapes aside. These will be used by students only if they request them.

Figure 1-2

Distribution center

LESSON 1

15. You may wish to divide the lesson into two sessions. An appropriate stopping point is suggested before the **Final Activities.**

Management Tip: Some students may not want to continually disassemble or modify their vehicles. To help students move on to the next design, you can create a record of their vehicles by photographing them as they are completed. You may also want to photograph the students themselves while they build and test their vehicles. The photographs can be included in a portfolio, as suggested in the Additional Assessments (pgs. 173–84).

Procedure

1. Introduce the unit by asking students to think about vehicles and what causes them to move. Ask students to think about how engineers design vehicles. Let students know they will investigate their ideas by designing, building, and testing the motion of vehicles throughout this unit.

2. Have students pick up their science notebooks, loose-leaf paper, and graph paper from the distribution center. (They will pick up the buckets later.) Let students know that scientists and engineers keep journals detailing their investigations and observations. Like scientists and engineers, students will keep written records and drawings in their notebooks.

3. After students have placed the loose-leaf and graph paper in their notebooks, ask them to write their names on the notebooks and date the first page. Let students know they will use the loose-leaf paper for written observations and the graph paper for drawings. Discuss with the class the importance of dating each day's entry.

4. Direct students' attention to the sheet of newsprint titled "What We Know about the Motion and Design of Vehicles." Ask them to spend a few minutes independently writing their thoughts on this topic in their notebooks. (You may want them to first write about how vehicles move. Then they can write about how to design vehicles.)

5. Invite students to share their ideas in a brainstorming session. Using a colored marker, record their ideas on the list. (See Figure 1-3.) Put a check next to duplicate responses to acknowledge all contributions.

Management Tips

- If your class is large, you may want to divide it into groups of six for the brainstorming activity. If you do this, have one student from each group record the group's ideas on the class list.

- If possible, keep this brainstorming list displayed throughout the unit. Encourage students to use Post-it® notes to add comments to the list as the unit progresses.

6. Direct students' attention to the second sheet of newsprint titled "What We Want to Find Out about Motion and Design." Ask them to spend a few minutes independently writing their thoughts on this topic in their notebooks. Then hold a brainstorming session and record their ideas on the list. Put a check next to duplicate responses to acknowledge all contributions.

7. Divide the students into groups of three and assign each group its letter. Ask groups to decide on work roles for each group member.

8. Ask a member from each group to collect a labeled bucket of building pieces from the distribution center. Let students know the letter on their buckets corresponds to their group letter. The letters will help them identify their buckets in future lessons.

Figure 1-3

Sample brainstorming list

9. Invite students to share what they discovered during their free exploration time with the building pieces, such as how the pieces connect. If students are having difficulty connecting the pieces, you can distribute one copy of **Tips on Using the Building Pieces** to each group. Students can refer to the tips throughout the unit.

Management Tip: If you decide to divide this lesson into two sessions, this is a good stopping point.

Final Activities

1. Let students know their first design challenge will be to meet the following requirements: In 20 minutes or less, design and build a vehicle (cart) that will move at least 100 cm (39 in). Before students begin building, ask them how they will test whether their vehicles meet the requirements.

2. Allow groups time to build their vehicles and test the designs.

Management Tips

- Note which groups request a measuring tape for measuring the distance their vehicles travel or a timer to keep track of the time requirement. You can use this information for the pre-unit assessment at the end of this lesson.

- Some groups may easily complete this design challenge in 20 minutes. Some may need more time or may have difficulty, for example, attaching wheels to the frame. Other groups may have built vehicles but cannot move them the 100 cm. Remind students that this lesson is simply for getting started and that they will have many opportunities throughout the unit to design, build, and test how vehicles move.

3. Ask students to spend a few minutes recording in their notebooks answers to the following questions:

- How did you get your vehicle to move?

- What was one problem your group encountered while building the vehicle? How did you solve the problem?

LESSON 1

4. Ask groups to finish by doing the following:

   - Label your vehicle with a small piece of masking tape marked with the group's letter.
   - Carefully place your completed vehicle on the distribution center. You will use the vehicle again in Lesson 2.
   - Return all extra building pieces and other materials to the group's bucket.
   - Place the inventory sheet **Building Pieces for Each Group** in the bucket.
   - Return the bucket to the distribution center.

Extensions

[SCIENCE] [ART]

1. Have students create a list of materials from home that they could use to build a vehicle. Spools of thread and lids from baby food jars work well for wheels. Empty, 1-liter (1-qt) cardboard milk cartons or cereal boxes can be used for a vehicle body. Have students select various materials from their lists, bring them in, and build their own vehicles.

[LANGUAGE ARTS]

2. Ask students to find a definition for the term "vehicle." Have them make a list of as many vehicles as they can think of.

[ART]

3. Ask students to connect two or three of the building pieces to make a simple construction. Now have them draw this construction. When they are finished, have students exchange their drawings with a partner and try to build their partner's construction from the drawing.

[SOCIAL STUDIES]

4. Have students research and write about the invention of the wheel in ancient civilizations.

Assessment

Each student's notebook entries, responses during the brainstorming sessions, and constructed vehicle from this lesson will enable you to assess his or her knowledge about motion and design and the processes the group used to meet a design challenge. This information serves as the first part of the matched pre- and post-unit assessments, both of which are integral to teaching the unit. The post-unit assessment (pgs. 169–71) follows Lesson 16.

To help you keep track of information about each student, record informal observations on charts, cards, or notes. If you decide to photograph the vehicles constructed in each lesson, label the photographs with the corresponding group letter and lesson number. As you review class brainstorming lists, individual notebook entries, work products, and classroom activities, keep the following criteria in mind for each student.

Brainstorming Session

- What does the student already know about how vehicles move?
- What does the student already know about design and engineering?
- Has the student had experience building, designing, or testing? (for example, a house built of cards, a mobile, a model volcano)

LESSON 1

Notebook Entries

When you review students' notebook entries from the brainstorming session, look for answers to the following questions:

- How detailed are the entries?
- Do the entries reflect oral contributions made by the student during the brainstorming session? Do the entries reflect other ideas as well?

When you review students' notebook entries from the close of the lesson, look for the following:

- Does the student use words or drawings to describe the motion of his or her vehicle? For example, a student's initial descriptions may include observations such as "I pushed the vehicle and it rolled" or "Our wheels were stuck. The car didn't move very far."
- In meeting the design challenge, does the student demonstrate an ability to recognize and solve problems?

Work Products and Process Skills

- Does the student recognize a need for and use a measuring tool to record the distance the vehicle moves?
- Can the student test and reevaluate the vehicle during construction? For example, does the student notice that the wheels do not rotate? Does the student remove the wheels and reattach them until they do?
- Can the student manipulate the materials in such a way as to meet the design requirements?

Drawings

In Lesson 2, students will draw the vehicles they built in this lesson. You can use their drawings as a pre-unit assessment and a standard for comparison with drawings made later in the unit. See Lesson 2's **Assessment** (pgs. 35–36) for more information.

The section **Teaching *Motion and Design*** (pgs. 6–16) includes a detailed discussion about the assessment of student learning. The specific goals and related assessments for this unit are summarized in Figure T-2 (pgs. 9–13). Some fourth-graders may not completely understand every concept and goal listed. As you observe individuals in your class, look for the development of these ideas and skills rather than their mastery.

Preparation for Lesson 12

- Students should not disassemble their vehicles at the end of Lesson 1. They will draw the vehicles in Lesson 2.
- Remind students not to make changes to their vehicles between lessons. Let them know they will have plenty of opportunities to alter the design of their vehicles as the unit progresses.

Blackline Master

Building Pieces for Each Group

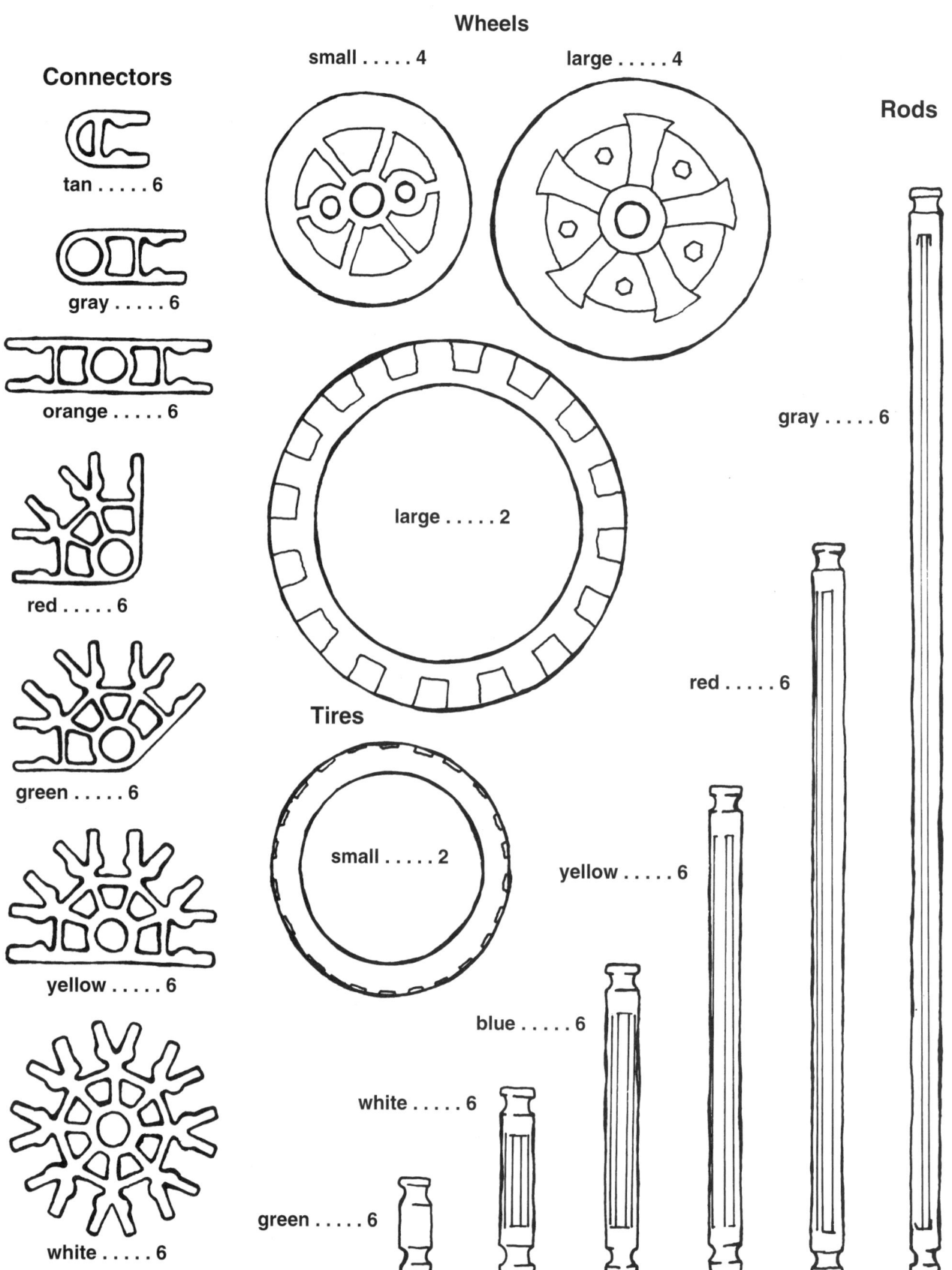

STC / *Motion and Design*

Tips on Using the Building Pieces

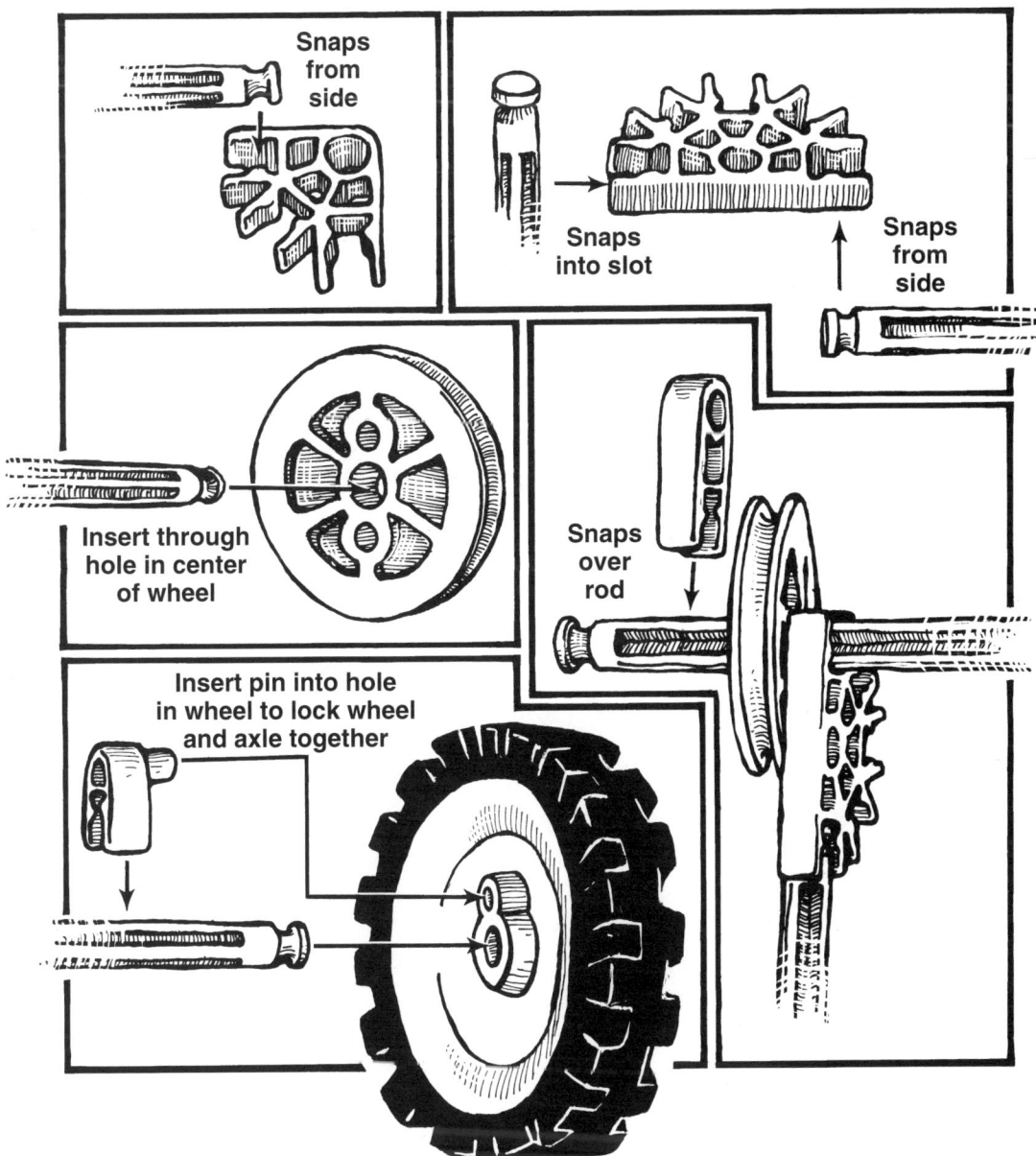

LESSON 2

Using Drawings to Record and Build

Overview and Objectives

In this lesson, students focus on the use of drawings in the design process. They begin by drawing the vehicles they built in Lesson 1. Then they use their visual and spatial perception skills to build a "standard" vehicle as pictured in a technical drawing. When students compare their own drawings with the technical drawing and analyze the techniques used to create each one, they learn that drawings can be used by others to replicate a design. In future lessons, students will use the standard vehicles built in this lesson to test the effects of force on motion.

- Students make a record of the vehicles they built in Lesson 1.
- Students build a vehicle by following a two-view technical drawing.
- Students identify details that are important in technical drawings and compare their own drawings with a technical drawing.
- Students read to learn more about the challenges of technological design.

Background

Engineers prepare careful drawings of their designs. These drawings must be detailed enough that a builder can construct the product, ideally with no further guidance from the engineer. The details include the scale, materials, parts, and how the parts fit together. Engineers typically create a special set of technical drawings called a **three-view drawing.** This set of drawings shows an object from three perspectives: top, side, and front. These perspectives can be difficult to interpret, however, because they appear so unlike the object.

In the past, engineers used drawing instruments such as a ruler, compass, and T square. Today, engineers use computers. Computer simulations can quickly create drawings that reveal depth, height, and width and make objects readily recognizable. Engineers can rotate these three-dimensional drawings on the computer screen to see all sides of the object. Computer-aided design programs are available that can check for the accuracy and integration of the various technical drawings in a design project.

In the first half of this lesson, students draw the vehicles they built in Lesson 1. They will probably combine in one drawing several perspectives of their vehicle. You may see, for example, the frame of the vehicle represented by a rectangle (top view) and the wheels represented by circles or disks (side view). Future lessons will provide students with opportunities to improve their drawing. This will help them draw each part of the vehicle from the same perspective and enable them to use the drawings as design plans.

LESSON 2

In the second half of the lesson, students follow a technical drawing to build standard vehicles. This technical drawing shows the top and side views of a simple vehicle constructed from the building pieces. Notice that the side view shows only two wheels. If you were to put this vehicle on a tabletop at eye level to get a side view, you would see at least three wheels and usually four. Only if you stood very far away would the vehicle begin to resemble the drawing. The drawing is actually a **mathematical construction**—a representation of how the vehicle would appear to an observer looking at it from a particular perspective and a far distance.

Even with the simple vehicles that students construct in this lesson, drawing and interpreting the various views is challenging. Be prepared to provide plenty of time and encouragement. Try not to dictate instructions to students, which can deny them the opportunity to solve the problems independently. Ask questions that will develop students' thinking and problem-solving skills. Encourage them to solve the problems independently or through collaboration with their peers.

Materials

For each student
1 science notebook (with loose-leaf and graph paper)
1 pencil with eraser

For each group of three students
1 vehicle (from Lesson 1)
1 bucket of building pieces
1 set of colored pencils (to match the building pieces)
1 circle template
1 metric ruler

For the class
   Brainstorming list, "What We Know about the Motion and Design of Vehicles" (from Lesson 1)
1 fine-point permanent marker
   Masking tape
1 Post-it® notepad, 7.6 × 12.7 cm (3 × 5 in)
   Bucket of extra building pieces

Preparation

1. To familiarize yourself with the activities in this lesson, you may want to do the following before starting the lesson:

   - Draw (on graph paper) a diagram of one group's vehicle from Lesson 1.
   - Refer to Figure 2-2 (pg. 35 in this guide and pg. 7 in the Student Activity Book) and assemble a vehicle.

2. Place a Post-it® notepad near the class brainstorming list displayed from Lesson 1. Students can use these notes throughout the unit to post additional comments or questions on the list.

3. Arrange the buckets, colored pencils, rulers, circle templates, and the vehicles from Lesson 1 at a distribution center.

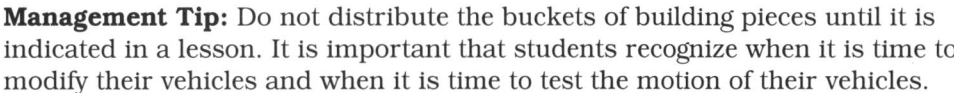

Procedure

1. Refer students to the brainstorming list from Lesson 1, "What We Know about the Motion and Design of Vehicles." Ask students to identify statements that relate to drawing or to design plans. Let students know that engineers use science and math to plan, design, and construct products. They often sketch their ideas and plans *before* they build. They also make detailed records of their products *after* building them, either by drawing them or using computer graphics, so the products can be studied and improved. Let students know they will do similar activities in this lesson.

2. Guide students in getting their vehicles, colored pencils, rulers, and circle templates from the distribution center. Tell them they will pick up their buckets later.

Management Tip: Do not distribute the buckets of building pieces until it is indicated in a lesson. It is important that students recognize when it is time to modify their vehicles and when it is time to test the motion of their vehicles.

3. Ask students to draw their group's vehicle from Lesson 1 on graph paper. If any group was unable to build a vehicle in Lesson 1, have that group make a simple construction from the building pieces and then draw it. Remind students to date their drawings. For pre-unit assessment purposes, note which students use the circle templates for drawing wheels, which students use the ruler for drawing straight lines, and which students use color and labels. If some students are initially uncomfortable with drawing, allow them to write a description of their vehicle in addition to drawing it.

Figure 2-1

Making a two-view drawing

LESSON 2

Management Tip: Colored pencils that match the various building pieces are provided in the kit. Students can use their own gray pencils for drawing the gray rods.

4. After students record their designs on graph paper, let them know they now have a permanent record of their designs. Ask students to pick up their buckets from the distribution center, disassemble their vehicles, and return all building pieces to their buckets. Remind students that their drawings can serve as a way of remembering what they built.

5. Allow time for students to analyze their drawings and descriptions. Prompt them to think about how they could use the drawing as a **blueprint,** or a detailed plan, by asking the following question: If you were to build the same vehicle again, what features on the drawing would make it easy to build?

6. Direct students' attention to the drawing of a vehicle (Figure 2-2, on pg. 35 in this guide and pg. 7 in the Student Activity Book). Let students know that each group will use this technical drawing to build a standard vehicle. Students will use standard vehicles in their investigations during the next six lessons.

7. Before students begin building, have them examine the technical drawing and decide which pieces they need to build the vehicle. The pieces needed are as follows:

2 tan hub connectors	2 gray rods
2 gray connectors	2 blue rods
4 red connectors	2 small wheels
4 yellow connectors	2 large wheels
2 red rods	2 large tires

   If students have difficulty following the technical drawing, encourage them to look at the labels. They can also use colored pencils to color their technical drawing before they begin building.

8. Allow time for students to build their vehicles.

Final Activities

1. Ask students to display their completed vehicles. If all of the vehicles are identical, ask students to explain why.

2. Have students compare their own drawings with the technical drawing. Prompt a discussion with questions such as the following:

   - How is your own drawing similar to or different from the technical drawing?
   - On the technical drawing, what do you notice about the two views of the vehicle? How are they alike? How are they different?
   - What parts of the technical drawing might make it easy for you to build this vehicle? What parts might make it difficult?
   - How does color help in a drawing?
   - Which drawing (your own or the technical one) might be easier to use if you needed to build 100 copies of a single model? Why?

3. Ask each group to use the fine-point permanent marker to write its group letter on a small piece of masking tape and then to wrap it around an axle of the vehicle they just built. Have students return their vehicles and other materials to the distribution center. Students can store their colored pencils, circle template, and ruler in their buckets.

Figure 2-2

Technical drawing of a vehicle

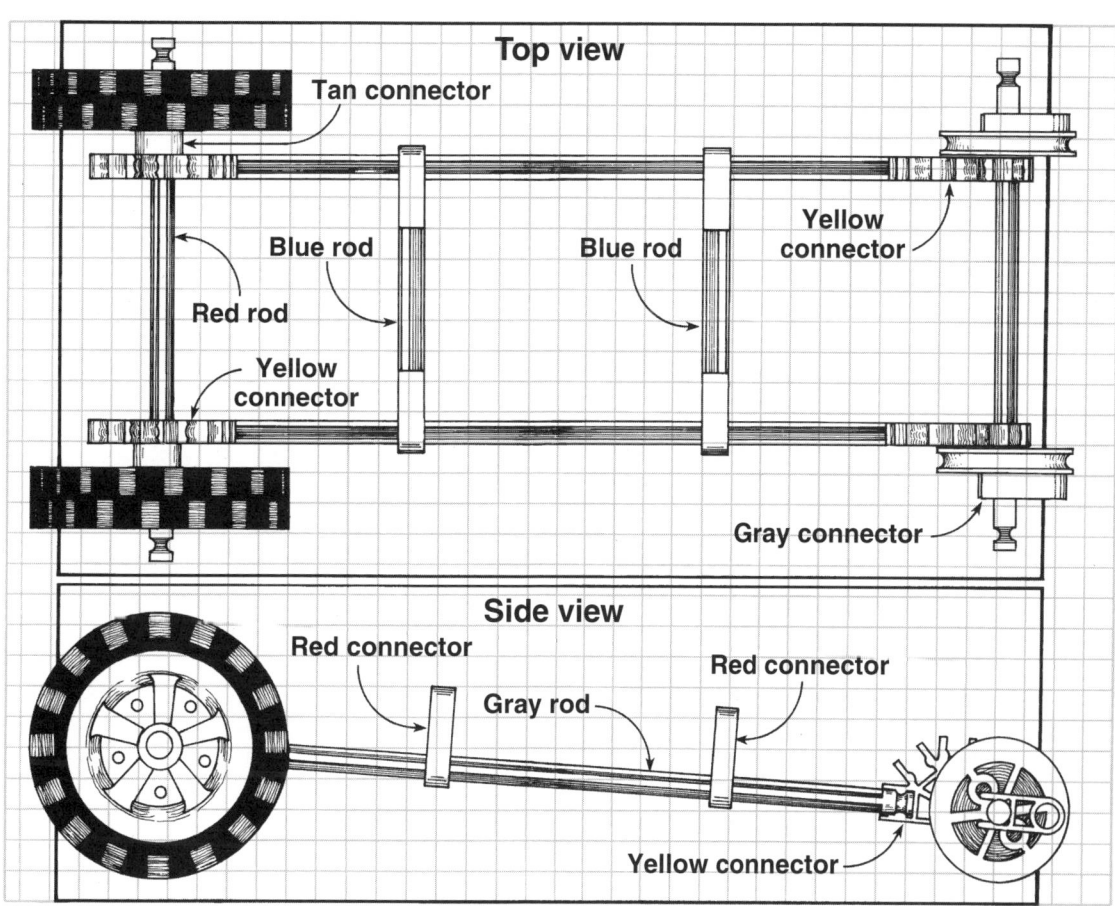

Management Tip: The following step can be completed now or at another time, such as during language arts.

4. Group students in pairs and have them read "The Race That Wasn't Run" (pgs. 37–39 in this guide and pgs. 9–11 in the Student Activity Book). As students read the selection, ask them to think about how they felt while building their vehicles in Lesson 1. How might their feelings be similar to what Bobby Rahal and his design team experienced?

Extensions

1. Arrange a learning center in which you place a circle template (and other kinds of templates), rulers, graph paper, colored pencils, and extra building pieces. Encourage students to build objects at the learning center and to practice recording their designs with drawings.

2. Invite students to bring in photographs, magazine cutouts, or drawings that show particular views of an object or person—front, side, or top. Have students sort the pictures on the basis of their perspective.

LESSON 2

ART

3. Ask each group to have one student pose while the other two draw two or three views (front, side, top) of the first student's head. Ask students where they have seen photographs like their drawings (profile shots, silhouettes, "Wanted" posters). Have them draw an object, such as a desk, book, or flower, from several perspectives.

LANGUAGE ARTS

4. Place an object in a place where everyone can see it. Now ask volunteers to walk around the object and describe, in writing, how it looks from different directions. Ask which view or views provide the most useful information.

ART

5. Ask students to hold a pencil at arm's length with the point facing toward them. Ask them to draw what they see. Now have them set the pencil on a desk and look down on it from above. Again have them draw what they see.

MATHEMATICS **SOCIAL STUDIES**

6. Challenge students to find out what a scale drawing is. Ask them to look at their vehicles and their vehicle drawings. Is the vehicle drawn to scale (all parts in proportion)? For example, are the wheels the correct size when compared with the body of the vehicle? Students can also find a scale on maps. Have them use the scale to calculate actual distances between cities.

Assessment

As stated in Lesson 1, you may want to use this lesson as a way of preassessing your students' abilities to record designs through drawing. Establish a basis for identifying growth in drawing skills throughout the unit by answering the following questions:

- How closely does the student look at the object he or she draws?
- How well does the student understand the way the building pieces fit together?
- Does the student effectively communicate the vehicle's design?
- Does the student use labels, colors, or other means to create a clear drawing of the vehicle?
- In what ways does the student show perspective in the drawing? Does the student's drawing include only one view or are several views shown in one drawing?
- What tools—including graph paper, circle template, ruler, and colored pencils—does the student use when recording designs? Look for improvement in using these tools as the unit progresses.

Keep in mind that the overall goal is not for students to master technical drawing but to show improvement in the way they build from and record designs.

Preparation for Lesson 3

- To save time during Lesson 3, you may want to prepare the strings and paper clip hooks ahead of time. See the directions in Lesson 3, Preparation Step 3 (pg. 43).
- Students should not alter their vehicles between Lessons 2 and 3.

Reading Selection

The Race That Wasn't Run

Indy car

How did you feel when you were building your vehicle in Lesson 1? Did you have any problems? Were you able to get the wheels to roll? Did the vehicle move like you wanted it to? Maybe you thought, "If only I had more time, I know I could get this to work better." Often that may be true. But sometimes we just don't have more time. Sometimes we have to stop working on a project even when we would like to keep improving it. World-famous race car driver Bobby Rahal (say "Ray-hall") had an experience like that when he designed and built his own "Indy car."

Indy cars are the sleek, powerful race cars that compete in the Indianapolis 500, among other races. The "Indy 500," as this 500-mile (805-km) race is called, takes place on Memorial Day in Indianapolis, Indiana, each year. About half a million people go to see it. The best drivers in the world compete there.

The illustration shows what an Indy car looks like. As you can see, the front end resembles the nose of an airplane. This shape helps increase speed. The car also has "wings" at the front and back to help air flow around it.

Most Indy cars are made by a company in England. Few racers have tried to build their own. So why did Bobby Rahal and his partner, Carl Hogan, want to build an Indy car? The challenge appealed to them and their company, Rahal/Hogan Racing. Bobby Rahal had already won the Indy 500 in 1986. But in 1992, Rahal decided he wanted to race a special car—one that he and his design team would design and build themselves. It would be the only car of its kind in the world.

LESSON 2

In Lesson 1, you were part of a design team that built a vehicle. Rahal/Hogan Racing had a design team, too. It included engineers, computer specialists, and a race car aerodynamicist, someone who knows how the airflow around a car affects its speed and performance. The team had seven months to design, build, and test the car before the 1993 Indy 500.

To be competitive at the Indy 500, Rahal's car would need to travel about 220 miles (354 km) per hour. How fast is that? If you stood on the sideline of a football field and watched a car drive from one end of the field to the other at 220 miles per hour, you would see only a blur. At that speed, it would take the car 1 second to make the trip down the field.

The Indy 500 is run on an oval-shaped track that has curved corners as well as straightaways. The cars go around this 2½-mile (4-km) track 200 times in the 500-mile race. Since they can go around the track in about a minute's time, they are turning one corner after another within seconds of each other. If a car loses speed on the corners, it can lose the race. Bobby's design team knew they faced a big challenge—to design a car that would move at high speeds and also grip the track around the corners.

After weeks of building, testing, and modifying the Indy car, an unexpected problem arose during a test run on a track in Phoenix, Arizona. As Bobby entered a turn at

about 170 miles (274 km) per hour, the back end of the car swung out and hit the guard wall. The car was not badly damaged, and Bobby was only shaken up. But the problem was serious. The car was unstable in the corners at unpredictable moments. The design team had a new challenge—to find the cause of the problem and fix it.

The design team worked day and night looking for a defective part or a poorly designed feature. They redesigned the rear wing of the car and ran tests of it in a wind tunnel. They revised the front wing. They tried every change they could think of and practically built a new car in the process. Sometimes they seemed to be close to a solution, but then the car would suddenly become unstable again, swinging out toward the wall.

Finally, they had to stop working. It was time for all the drivers who wanted to race in the 1993 Indy 500 to try to qualify. In the qualifying runs, the drivers take turns racing around the track. Only the fastest cars get to compete in the actual race.

Can you imagine how the design team felt as they watched Bobby drive onto the track? How they must have wished they had more time. How they must have hoped everything would go perfectly. How they must have hoped Bobby would qualify for the Indy 500 and then win it.

But do you know what happened? Everything did not go perfectly. The car became unstable, and it never quite reached the speed needed to qualify. Bobby Rahal would not race in the Indy 500.

At trackside, the Rahal/Hogan design team was stunned. They had put all their effort into the project, and time had run out. As disappointed as he was, Bobby spoke to reporters before leaving the speedway. "It's going to be an odd Memorial Day for me not being in this race. But we'll be back next year. We'll go get 'em again." He thanked the fans for their support. Then he left the track.

Even after seven months of hard work, the team could not solve the car's flaw. It was not easy to set aside this project when the team had put such effort into it. But there was nothing more they could do.

When one challenge ends, often there is another one just ahead. Bobby Rahal did not build a successful car for the 1993 Indy 500. But he never gave up on racing or winning. In fact, not long after the 1993 racing season, Bobby Rahal's design team began working on a new Indy car engine.

Derived, with permission, from *Fast Cars*, a NOVA® production by Cambridge Studios for WGBH Boston, in association with Sveriges TV. © 1995 WGBH Educational Foundation. (Teachers and educational institutions may purchase this NOVA® videocassette or video teaching modules. Call 1-800-255-9424.)

LESSON 3

Pulling a Vehicle: Looking at Force

Overview and Objectives

Lessons 1 and 2 introduced students to building vehicles and recording their designs. This lesson focuses on force and motion and allows students to develop an understanding of the principle that force applied to an object changes the motion of that object. To ensure a fair test, students use the standard vehicles built in Lesson 2 and set up a system in which a falling weight attached to a string pulls the vehicle. This activity provides an opportunity for students to describe in detail how their vehicles respond to this pull. The lesson also sets the stage for a more formal collection and graphing of data in Lesson 4.

- Students set up a system to pull their vehicles.
- Students compare and discuss how the motion of their vehicles changes when more or less weight on a string is used to pull them.
- Students record their observations in writing.
- Students draw conclusions about the effect of differently weighted strings on the motion of their string-pulled vehicles.

Background

To move a vehicle at rest requires a **force**—a push or a pull. Similarly, to slow or stop a moving vehicle also requires a force. **Unbalanced forces** initiate and influence movement. Imagine a tug-of-war. As it begins, both sides pull with equal force. Suddenly, one player drops out. The advantage moves toward the side with the stronger force. The speed of the rope and the players increases in the direction of the stronger force.

Newton's first law of motion states that when a force is exerted on an object, the force acts to increase the speed of that object, to change its direction, or to slow or stop its motion. The effect of the force on the motion of the object depends on the size and direction of the force.

In the next three lessons, students tie a string to their vehicles, hang the string over the edge of a table, and attach weights (small washers) to the end of the string. The vehicle is pulled by the force of gravity, which acts on the weighted string and pulls the weights toward the floor. This unbalanced force on the vehicle causes it to move. The greater the force (that is, the greater the number of weights on the string), the greater the pull on the vehicle and the faster the vehicle changes its speed. Frequently, a vehicle will continue to move along the work space even after the falling weight has reached the floor and no longer exerts a pull on the vehicle. This continued motion is due to inertia. (To prevent

LESSON 3

their vehicles from rolling off the table and hitting the floor, students will create a barrier by placing a bookend at the end of their work space. See illustration on the Student Instruction Sheet, pgs. 47–48.)

When groups attach the weighted string to their vehicles, one student will pull back on the group's vehicle to hold it in place. The forces are balanced, and the vehicle will not move. The student will be able to feel the pull of the weights on his or her hand through the vehicle. When the student lets go, the forces become unbalanced and the vehicle moves in the direction of the pull. Help students recognize that forces are acting on their vehicles even when they are not moving.

Once the vehicle is in motion, it will remain in motion until another force affects it. **Friction** is the force that opposes motion. In this lesson, friction occurs between the wheels and the axle as they rub together, and between the wheels and tires and the surface over which the vehicle moves. After the weighted string stops pulling, friction will slow and stop the forward motion of the vehicle. Students will study friction in more detail in Lesson 8.

Materials

For each student
- 1 science notebook

For each group of three students
- 1 copy of **Record Sheet 3-A: Recording How Our Vehicle Moves**
- *1 standard vehicle (labeled with group letter, from Lesson 2)
- 1 piece of string, 100 cm (39 in)
- 1 piece of cardboard, 23 × 30 cm (9 × 12 in)
- 2 jumbo paper clips
- 16 small metal washers
- 1 large metal washer
- 1 large bookend with nonslip base, 23h × 15w × 20d cm (9h × 6w × 8d in), about 0.5 kg (1 lb)
- 1 strip of Masonite™, 38 × 122 × 0.6 cm (15 × 48 × ¼ in), or foamboard, 38 × 122 × 0.5 cm (15 × 48 × 3/16 in) (optional)

For the class
- 10 small plastic cups, 30 ml (1 oz)
- 1 spool of light string
- 1 measuring tape, 100 cm (39 in)
- Scissors
- Masking tape

*The term *standard vehicle* will be used throughout the unit to refer to the vehicles students built in Lesson 2 using a technical drawing.

Preparation

Management Tip: Consider soliciting the help of an adult volunteer for preparing this lesson. It is not recommended that students prepare the strings with paper clip hooks (see **Preparation** Step 3), since they may not have the fine motor skills to manipulate these materials.

1. Decide whether, in this lesson and throughout the unit, students will complete the record sheet as a group or individually. Make one copy of **Record Sheet 3-A: Recording How Our Vehicle Moves** for each group (or student).

2. For each group, assign a long, flat work area off the floor such as the following:

   - a rectangular or square table in the classroom,
   - a table in the library or cafeteria, or
   - a Masonite™ or foamboard "runway" placed over two or more student desks of equal height, or over a round table. (The falling-weight system requires a straight table edge.)

Management Tip: Masonite™ can be purchased and cut at your local hardware store. Foamboard is available at office or art supply stores. It can be cut with a utility knife into pieces measuring 38 × 122 cm (15 × 48 in). You can order a precut set of foamboard strips for *Motion and Design* from Carolina Biological Supply Company. Cover one of the 38-cm (15-in) cut edges of the board with masking tape. This will ensure that the string does not catch on the edge when the weight falls.

3. Prepare a string with paper clip hooks for each group, as follows:

   - Cut the string into 100-cm (39-in) lengths. Each group needs one string.
   - Bend each paper clip into an S shape, like a hook. Each group needs two hooks.
   - Attach a hook to each end of the string. Tie and knot the hooks on the string, as shown in Figure 3-1.
   - Wrap each group's string around a piece of cardboard so it does not tangle. Use a small piece of masking tape to tape the hooks to the cardboard. (You will use the cardboard again in later lessons.)

Figure 3-1

Attaching paper clip hooks to the string

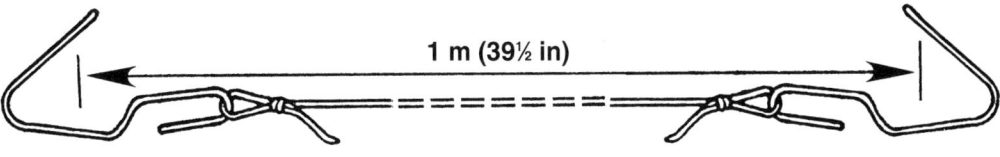

4. Place 16 small washers in each of the plastic cups. Each groups needs one cup.
5. Arrange the materials at the distribution center, as shown in Figure 3-2.
6. Use the **Student Instructions for Setting Up a Falling-Weight System** (pgs. 47–48 in this guide and pgs. 15–16 in the Student Activity Book) to set up one group's falling-weight system at the front of your classroom. You will use it as a demonstration when you review with students the setup and procedures for this lesson.

Procedure

1. Invite a student to move from one end of the room to another. Have the class describe the student's motion. Ask the student to move again, this time showing a change in motion (for example, walk and then run). Ask the class to describe the student's change in motion. Let the class know they will describe motion and *changes* in motion in this lesson and throughout the unit.

2. As students follow along, go over the **Student Instructions for Setting Up a Falling-Weight System** (pgs. 47–48 in this guide and pgs. 15–16 in the Student Activity Book). Ask a student volunteer to demonstrate the investigation using the falling-weight system you set up at the front of the room. Ask students to speculate about the purpose of the bookend.

LESSON 3

Figure 3-2

Distribution center

3. Distribute **Record Sheet 3-A: Recording How Our Vehicle Moves.** Let students know that for each set of weights they test (four sets in all), they are to record the motion and changes in motion of their vehicles. Review with students the example shown on the record sheet.

4. Ask students to pick up their vehicles and other materials from the distribution center. Remind them to carefully unwrap their string from the cardboard so it does not tangle.

5. Have students set up their falling-weight systems and complete the investigation.

Final Activities

1. Have students share their findings. Encourage discussion by asking questions such as the following:

   - When did you observe your vehicle begin to move?
   - What caused your vehicle to move?
   - Did the vehicle move differently when you changed the weight? Why do you think this happened?
   - What made the vehicle stop moving each time?
   - Why did you use the bookend? Did you need it each time? Why or why not?
   - For each different weight you used, how would you describe the motion of the vehicle?

2. Discuss the speed rankings on the record sheets. Ask students to describe how the amount of force affects the motion of their vehicles.

   Note: Your students may say, "More weight on the string (or a greater force) made the vehicle move faster." This is acceptable, but help them understand that the greater the force, the greater the change in speed over the same distance. One way to describe this change in speed is, "The vehicle got going more quickly with more weight" or "A bigger pull made the vehicle take off faster."

3. Discuss the Thinking Challenge on **Record Sheet 3-A.** Help students recognize that their vehicles moved a distance equal to the height of their work spaces. Discuss why this is so.

4. Have students clean up by returning their vehicles and other materials to the distribution center. Ask them to carefully wrap their string around the cardboard so it does not tangle. Have students return the 16 small washers to the plastic cups. They will use the string with hooks and the washers in Lesson 4.

Extensions

SCIENCE

1. Ask students to form pairs, take turns moving, and take turns describing each other's motion. Students can move across a room, hallway, gym floor, or playground. Then challenge partners to observe changes in motion, for example, slowing down, speeding up, and changing direction. Students can create motion cards with a different speed description on each card (for example, "Not moving," "Moving slowly"). One partner can lay the cards out to create a sequential speed description. The other partner must move according to that sequence.

Figure 3-3

Looking at changes in motion

LESSON 3

SCIENCE

2. Ask students to find examples of objects that move by the force of gravity. Examples include apples falling from trees, rocks tumbling down a hillside, and a wagon rolling downhill. Or have them find examples of moving objects attached to a rope. Examples include a bucket suspended in a well, window washers hoisting themselves up and down the side of a building with ropes, a pulley system in an auto mechanic's shop or on a boat, and the weights in a grandfather clock. Students may be interested in researching the Volcano Rover, a robot attached to a tether that is used to explore volcanoes.

MATHEMATICS

3. Have students use a balance to compute how many small washers are equal to the weight of 1 large washer. Did all students come up with the same equivalency? Why might differences occur? Ask students to find other objects that have a weight equivalent to 2, 4, 8, or 16 small washers.

SCIENCE

4. Have the class play tug-of-war with adult supervision. Conduct the following investigation and discussion. Begin with just one student on each side. Add one student at a time to either side. Do the pulls (forces) remain balanced? Does the center marker move? Why or why not? When each side has an equal number of students, begin randomly adding or removing students. Observe the direction in which the center marker moves. What determines the direction in which the rope moves? Have students explain why the rope might not move at all, even though students on both sides are pulling.

SCIENCE   **MATHEMATICS**

5. Ask students to set up a falling-weight investigation in which a rubber band, not a paper clip, connects the string to the vehicle. Remind them to wear safety goggles. Have them observe what happens to the rubber band when they add the weights. What happens to the rubber band when they release the vehicle? What happens to the rubber band when the weights reach the floor? What can they conclude from these observations? Have students increase the number of weights on the string and make additional observations. Students can measure how far the rubber band stretches with each trial. (Help students realize that the stretched rubber band is a visual indication that the weights are pulling on the vehicle the entire time—from the moment they are attached to the vehicle to the moment they reach the floor.)

Preparation for Lesson 4

Students should not disassemble their standard vehicles. They will use them again in Lesson 4.

LESSON 3

Student Instructions for Setting up a Falling-Weight System

Directions: Pick up your materials. Place your vehicle on the long, flat work space assigned to your group by the teacher. Then set up the work space just as it is pictured.

1. Make certain to thread the string through the opening in the bookend. Have one member pull the vehicle back until the top of the paper clip hook lines up with the top edge of the table. If you are using a long board, pull the vehicle back until the rear wheels are near the end of the board. (Make certain the wheels remain on the board.)

2. While one member holds the vehicle in place, have another member put two small washers on the paper clip hook at edge of the table. Can the person who is holding the vehicle feel this added weight?

LESSON 3

3. Now let go of the vehicle. If the vehicle does not move, it may help to tap it *very slightly*. (If it still does not move, you will record that information on your record sheet.)

4. Discuss what you observed. Have the third member record your group's observations on **Record Sheet 3-A: Recording How Our Vehicle Moves.**

5. Pull your vehicle back again until the top of the paper clip hook lines up with the top edge of the table. Place two more small washers on the hook (four total). Discuss what it feels like to hold the vehicle in place with four washers on the hook.

6. Let go of the vehicle. Record your findings on the record sheet.

7. Pull the vehicle back again. Place four more small washers on the hook (eight total). Before you let go, discuss how it feels to hold the vehicle in place with eight washers on the hook. Then make a prediction. Discuss how the vehicle will move. Now let go of the vehicle. Record your findings.

8. Repeat this activity with 16 washers (or 1 large washer).

9. Now complete all of Record Sheet 3-A. Rank the speed of your vehicle when pulled by each weight by assigning each trial a number from one to five, with five being the fastest. Which weight pulled the vehicle the fastest?

LESSON 3

Record Sheet 3–A

Names: _____

_____

Date: _____

_____

Recording How Our Vehicle Moves

Number and Size of Washers	Observations about How the Vehicle Moved	Ranking the Speed (1–5) 1=slowest 5=fastest
1 small washer	There was only a small force pulling the car. First it wouldn't start moving. Then it moved very slowly.	
2 small washers		
4 small washers		
8 small washers		
16 small washers (or 1 large washer)		

Thinking Challenge: Think about the height of your work space and the length of your string. Think about the distance your vehicle moves. How are all these measurements related? Why?

_____

_____

_____

_____

STC / *Motion and Design*

LESSON 4

Testing the Motion of Vehicles Carrying a Load

Overview and Objectives

Applying what they learned from their observations in Lesson 3, students adapt their vehicles in this lesson to carry a load and test how the weight of the load affects the vehicles' motion. Using a constant force and varying the load, students grasp the idea that the heavier the vehicle, the slower its average speed. Through this investigation, students gain valuable experience in conducting a controlled experiment while developing their intuitive understanding of the role of mass in motion.

- Students add blocks to their vehicles to investigate the effects of a load on motion.
- Students measure the time it takes for a loaded vehicle to move a given distance.
- Students discuss and graph their results and observations.

Background

In Lesson 3, students made no changes to their vehicles and observed what happened when they varied the force acting on the vehicle. In this lesson, they keep the force constant and observe what happens when they vary the mass of their vehicles.

Mass is the amount of material in an object. **Weight** is the amount of force gravity exerts on an object's mass. On the Moon, people weigh one-sixth as much as on Earth, but their mass is the same. The mass of a vehicle is proportional to, but not the same as, the vehicle's weight.

The goal of Lessons 3 and 4 is to help students develop an understanding of the relationships among force, mass, and change in motion. It is not necessary to use the term *mass* in your discussions. Rather, help familiarize students with the way forces affect the motion of lighter and heavier vehicles.

Students will vary the mass of their vehicles by changing the number of wooden blocks they carry. They will discover that the larger the load, the more slowly the vehicle speeds up when a constant force is applied. The smaller the load, the more quickly the vehicle speeds up. This is a plausible result. For example, if a shopper pushes an empty grocery cart, it speeds up readily, whereas a full cart speeds up much more slowly. The larger load has more mass, and therefore more inertia, requiring a greater force to get it moving than if the load were small.

By using timers to measure the elapsed time of travel in seconds, students can quantify their investigation. Most timers or stopwatches have three buttons, which may cause some initial confusion for students. You may want to determine your students' skill in using timers before teaching this lesson. Follow the directions on the manufacturer's packaging when instructing students about the use of the timers. Also decide how you want students to read the timers. For example, they can read and record the elapsed time to the nearest whole second (large display) or to the nearest 1/100 second (large and small displays). The line plot on **Record Sheet 4-A** indicates only whole numbers. If you want students to measure and record more precisely, you will need to modify the record sheet or have students create their own line plots.

Even under seemingly identical conditions, groups may measure different elapsed times. Help students determine why this might be so. Are they starting their timers when the weight begins to fall and stopping them when the weight reaches the floor? Is friction affecting the vehicles during some trials? Are the wheels rubbing against the frame or is the paper clip hook dragging on the tabletop? Help students grasp what effects these variations, which are expected, might have.

Because of this variation, which is characteristic of all measurements, a single measurement has limited value for testing and evaluation. Therefore, students will be asked to repeat their measurements several times so that all the data can be used to obtain a representative value. With your students, you can decide how best to analyze the data. Following are some possibilities.

There are several ways to analyze students' data, including arithmetic mean, median, and mode. Adding the measurements and then dividing by the number of measurements to find the arithmetic **mean** may be the most familiar way for students to find an average. This approach, however, will result in a decimal average, which is inappropriate because it implies a level of accuracy that is not present in the measurements in this lesson. As explained below, either the **median** (middle measure) or the **mode** (most frequent measure) is more meaningful for this activity and easier to determine.

A **line plot** (see sample in Figure 4-1) will illustrate the range of students' measurements and allow them to decide which number or set of numbers best represents their data. A line plot shows the range of possible results on a horizontal axis. After each trial, students color a circle above the number on the line plot that represents the number of seconds it took their vehicles to travel a distance equal to the height of their work space while carrying a load of wooden blocks. The color of the circle corresponds to a given load. This color coding allows students to compare results for their vehicle when carrying various loads. In this investigation, the numbers on the horizontal axis are the number of seconds required for the vehicle to move a distance equal to the height of the work space.

The students who obtained the results in Figure 4-1 might say that the average time for their vehicle to travel a distance equal to the height of the work space while carrying zero blocks was "between one and two seconds." If they chose to analyze the data further, they might say that the mode was "about one second," since more colored circles lie above one second than above two seconds. When the vehicle carried one block, both the mode and the median were three seconds. Students might also conclude that the time it took the vehicle with one block to move a distance equal to the height of the work space was "somewhere around two to four seconds."

To help students recognize that measurements vary, you can ask questions, such as "About how much time did it take the vehicle to move a distance equal to the height of your work space?" You might also ask, "Which number is in the middle?" or "Which number of seconds happened most often with one block?" Encourage students to decide how they want to represent the average.

To maintain a constant force in this lesson, students use the same number of washers on the end of the string for all trials. If students changed both the load *and* the force, there would be no way to distinguish which variable affected the

Figure 4-1

Sample line plot

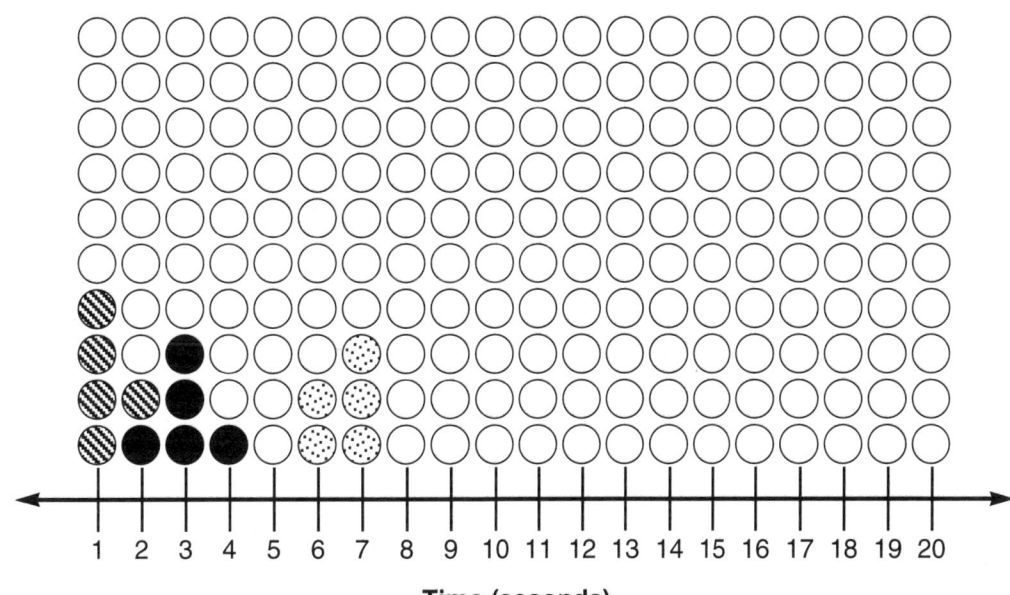

motion they observe. Therefore, it is suggested that students use at least 10 small washers as the constant force. Remind them that after they determine the number of washers for their group, they are not to vary the number on *any* of the trials.

The wood used in this unit is light enough that a vehicle carrying two blocks should move when pulled by 10 small washers. However, if a wooden block contains knots, it may be more dense, and thus heavier, than other blocks. If a group finds that their vehicle carrying two blocks will not move under the force of 10 small washers, ask the group to increase the number of washers one at a time until the vehicle does move. Once the appropriate number of washers is set, students *in that group* should record the number on their record sheet and keep this number of washers the same for each trial in this lesson.

If the height of each group's work space is the same, it will be easy to compare results among groups. However, if the height of the work spaces in your classroom differs, help students discover why results among the groups are different and why they cannot be compared.

Materials

For each student
  1 science notebook
  1 pencil with eraser

For each group of three students
  1 copy of **Record Sheet 4-A: Graphing Data**
  1 standard vehicle

LESSON 4

 1 string with paper clip hooks, wrapped around cardboard (from Lesson 3)
16 small metal washers in cup
 2 blocks of wood, 5 × 8 × 9 cm (2 × 3 × 3½ in)
 1 timer
 1 large bookend, with nonslip base, 23h × 15w × 20d cm (9h × 6w × 8d in), about 0.5 kg (1 lb)
 1 red colored pencil
 1 blue colored pencil
 1 green colored pencil
 1 strip of Masonite™, 38 × 122 × 0.6 cm (15 × 48 × ¼ in), or foamboard, 38 × 122 × 0.5 cm (15 × 48 × 3/16 in) (optional)

For the class

 1 spool of light string
 1 measuring tape, 100 cm (39 in)
 1 box of jumbo paper clips
   Scissors

Preparation

1. Make one copy of **Record Sheet 4-A: Graphing Data** for each group (or student).

2. Check each group's string (wrapped around cardboard) from Lesson 3. If any strings have become tangled or knotted or the hooks are missing, prepare and set out additional strings with hooks.

3. Set up work spaces, as you did in Lesson 3, where groups can work on a table or other elevated surface.

4. Arrange the materials at the distribution center, with the cardboard trays at the beginning. Each groups' 16 small washers should still be in the plastic cups.

5. Preview the lesson. Decide if you need one session or two to complete it. This will depend on your students' familiarity with using timers and line plots. An appropriate stopping point is suggested between **Procedure** Steps 9 and 10.

Procedure

1. Introduce the lesson by asking students to think about how adding blocks to their vehicles might change the way the vehicles move. Have students spend a few minutes writing predictions in their notebooks. Discuss their predictions.

2. Hold up one vehicle and two blocks of wood. Ask students how they could adapt their vehicles to hold two blocks of wood while moving. Accept all suggestions.

3. Let students know that to make this investigation a fair test, each group will attach the blocks in the same manner. Demonstrate the method, as shown in Figure 4-2. In Lesson 5, each group will have a chance to develop its own method.

4. Let students know that they will use a timer to measure how long it takes their vehicles to move in each trial. This will enable them to discuss and compare results. Distribute one timer to each group.

5. Give students a few minutes to explore starting and stopping the timer. Review the correct way to use the timer to measure elapsed time. Discuss what the large- and small-number displays on the timer represent.

Figure 4-2

Moving the crossbars to hold blocks

6. Have students time the motion of a student volunteer moving across the classroom. Let students know that for this investigation, they will round off their results to the nearest second. (See **Background** if you wish students to measure and record more precisely.)

7. Ask students to brainstorm examples of motion that we measure with time. Responses may include foot races, swimming meets, horse races, or car trips. Ask students to think about a 100-m (109-yd) dash in which one runner completes the race in 9 seconds and another in 12 seconds. Which runner moved faster? Make certain students understand that the shorter elapsed time indicates higher speed.

8. Review with students the **Student Instructions for Testing the Motion of Vehicles Carrying a Load** (pgs. 58–60 in this guide and pgs. 20–22 in the Student Activity Book).

9. Distribute and review **Record Sheet 4-A: Graphing Data.** An illustration on the Student Instruction Sheet and Figure 4-1 in the Background show a sample of a completed line plot. Make certain that students understand how to color the circles on the line plot.

Management Tip: If you need to divide this lesson into two sessions, this is a good stopping point.

LESSON 4

10. Guide students in getting their vehicles and other materials from the distribution center. Ask them to complete the investigation by following the student instructions on pgs. 58–60. Remind students to do the following:

    ■ Use the colored pencils to fill in the appropriate circles on the line plot on Record Sheet 4-A.

    ■ Keep the number of washers the same for each trial.

    ■ Change only the load carried by the vehicle.

Final Activities

1. Ask students to discuss their results. Use questions such as the following:

    ■ What did you observe when testing various loads (blocks)?

    ■ How did the vehicle move when it was loaded with two blocks?

    ■ How did the motion of the vehicle change when you removed one block? How did it change when you removed both blocks?

    ■ What do you think would happen if you added a third or fourth block to the vehicle?

    ■ When the vehicle carried no blocks, what was left to influence its motion? (the weight of the vehicle)

    ■ What can you conclude about the effects of load (such as blocks) on a vehicle's motion? (Help students understand that the heavier the vehicle, the longer the vehicle takes to respond to a force.)

    ■ What situations at home or in school may be similar to what you tested in this lesson?

2. Ask each group to refer to **Record Sheet 4-A: Graphing Data** and describe approximately how much time it took their vehicle in each trial to move the given distance. Help students understand that by taking repeated measurements and selecting a value from these measurements, they can get a more representative measure of the time it took their vehicle to move than if they measure only once. Some measurements (represented by colored circles) may cluster. Others may be spread out, in which case the middle circle can represent all of them. (See **Background** for more information on analyzing data.)

3. Ask students to return all materials to the distribution center. Make certain they carefully wrap their string around the cardboard so it does not tangle and return all washers to their cup. They will use the string with hooks and the washers again in Lesson 5.

Extensions

SCIENCE

1. Ask students to investigate how the position of the vehicle's load might affect their results. They might try blocks stacked horizontally instead of vertically, or a front-loading vehicle instead of a back-loading one.

MATHEMATICS

2. Have students use an equal-arm balance to find out how many blocks are equivalent to the weight of their vehicle. Ask them to discuss how this information helps them to understand the results of today's investigation.

LESSON 4

LANGUAGE ARTS

3. Ask students to imagine they are transporting an important shipment across the continent. What will the shipment be? What is the destination? Why must the shipment be delivered? How will they transport it? After they have delivered their load, how will the return trip be different?

MATHEMATICS

4. Have students use timers to measure the elapsed time of various events, such as the length of their lunch period, the amount of time it takes someone to run across the playground, the time it takes for a car to travel between two telephone poles, or how fast a fish swims the length of the fish tank.

SOCIAL STUDIES   **LANGUAGE ARTS**

5. Have students research and write about various load-bearing vehicles, including how they are different from each other.

ART

6. Invite students to display photographs of various load-bearing vehicles. Using materials from home, such as shoe boxes and empty spools, students can create a model of one of the displayed vehicles.

MATHEMATICS

7. Ask students to start their timers and stop them a few seconds later. Write down the elapsed time in decimal form. Now write the equivalent fraction.

Preparation for Lesson 5

Students should not disassemble their vehicles. They will modify the design of their standard vehicles in Lesson 5.

LESSON 4

Student Instructions for Testing the Motion of Vehicles Carrying a Load

1. Set up the falling-weight system as you did in Lesson 3.

2. Add two blocks to your vehicle. Squeeze the crossbars to make certain the blocks are held in place.

3. Make certain that one end of the string is attached to the vehicle and the other end is threaded through the opening in the bookend. Pull the vehicle back until the hook is at the top edge of your work space. Then have one group member hold the vehicle in place.

4. Place 10 small washers on the hook. Hang the weights over the edge of your work space (through the bookend). Make certain the hook is not stuck on the table edge.

5. Let go of the vehicle. If the vehicle does not move, tap it *lightly*. Can the 10 washers pull the vehicle?

6. If the vehicle still does not move at all, add more small washers, *one at a time*. Stop adding washers when the vehicle begins to move, even slightly, across the table.

7. Count your washers. Write the number on **Record Sheet 4-A.** Use this number of washers throughout this investigation. *Do not change* the number of washers.

8. Get your timer. Pull the vehicle back again until the hook is at the top edge of the table. When you are ready to begin, set the timer to 0.

9. As you let go of the vehicle, start the timer. (If the paper clip gets stuck on the edge of the table, start over.) Stop the timer when the falling weights touch the floor.

10. Now look at the large numbers on your timer. Use your **green** colored pencil. Color a circle at the bottom of the graph that matches the number of seconds it took your vehicle to move this distance.

11. Talk with your group about your vehicle's motion. How did the blocks affect how the weighted string pulled your vehicle?

12. Reset the timer to 0. Repeat these steps four more times with the vehicle carrying two blocks of wood. Reset your timer to 0 each time. After each trial, color a green circle on the graph to show your results. If you get the same time as an earlier trial, color a circle *directly above* the green circle from the other trial.

LESSON 4

13. Now remove one block from your vehicle. Squeeze the crossbars so the block stays in place. Pull the vehicle back until the hook is at the top edge of the table. Reset your timer to 0.

14. Let go of the vehicle. Stop the timer when the weights hit the floor. This time, show your results on the graph by coloring a circle **blue.** Do this five times altogether.

15. Remove the block from your vehicle. Now repeat the steps with an empty vehicle. Do this five times altogether. For these trials, use a **red** colored pencil to color the circles on the graph.

16. Now complete the bottom part of the record sheet.

Record Sheet 4-A

Names: _____

Date: _____

Graphing Data: How Load Affects the Time a Vehicle Travels

Number of washers we will use: _____

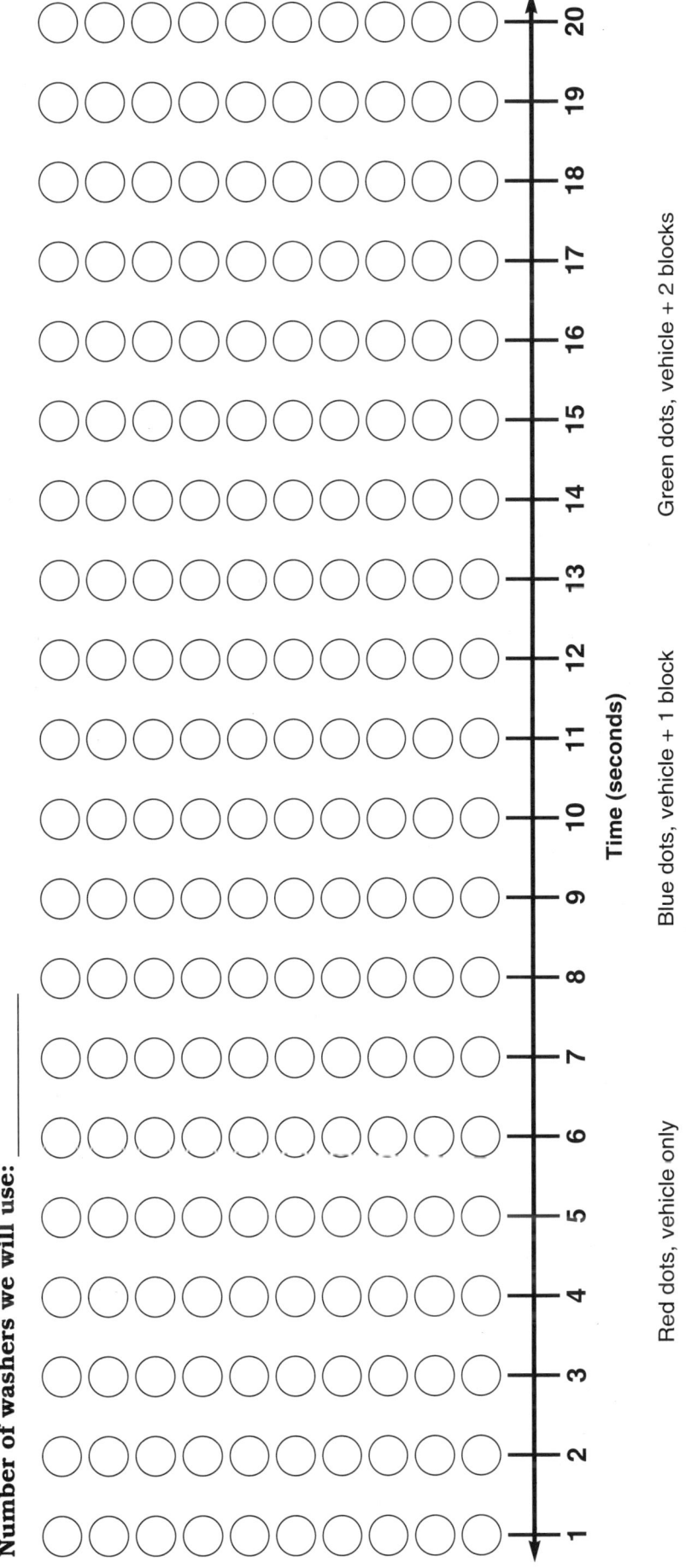

Now look at your dots. About how long did it take your vehicle to travel while carrying each of the following loads? (Pick the number in the middle of your five trials, or the number that has the most dots of one color.) Record the numbers below.

Vehicle only (red dots) _____ seconds

Vehicle + 1 block (blue dots) _____ seconds

Vehicle + 2 blocks (green dots) _____ seconds

STC / *Motion and Design*

LESSON 4

LESSON 5

Designing Vehicles to Meet Requirements

Overview and Objectives

In previous lessons, students gained experience in setting up systems to investigate the motion of vehicles and tested the effects of force and load on the vehicles' motion. In this lesson, students receive a design challenge: they must apply information collected in Lessons 3 and 4 to their own design of vehicles that move a specified distance in a specified amount of time. Students meet this challenge by using problem-solving skills to adjust the load on their vehicles, the force pulling the vehicles, and the weight of the vehicles themselves. As they modify the design of their vehicles by adding or removing pieces, students apply their knowledge of how weight and load affect a vehicle's motion.

- Students design vehicles and systems to pull the vehicles to meet time requirements.

- Students use and apply previously collected data to design their systems.

- Students read to learn more about a specialized vehicle, the Lunar Rover.

Background

In Lesson 3, students learned that a lighter weight on the end of the string produced slower vehicle motion. In Lesson 4, they learned that heavier loads carried by the vehicle produced slower changes in vehicle speed. Now they must apply both of these findings to meet a design requirement: The vehicle must move a distance equal to the height of the work space in four to six seconds.

Students' first inclination might be to use the heaviest load and the smallest number of washers in their system. However, they may find that as they increase the load to slow the vehicle, they must also add washers to the end of the string just to keep the vehicle moving. Likewise, if they reduce the number of washers, the vehicle may not move at all. This is an interesting problem for which there are many solutions. Several combinations of blocks and washers will meet the design requirement. In solving the challenge, students might also decide to add friction to their systems. For example, they might attach and drag washers from the rear of their vehicle to increase friction and reduce speed. Students might also grasp that the more building pieces they add to their vehicle, the greater the vehicle's weight and the more difficult it may be to get the vehicle moving.

Like engineers, students in this lesson plan, build, test, evaluate, modify, and retest their vehicles before presenting the results. By following a technological design process, they will apply scientific concepts to meet requirements. To plan and implement their investigation, students will need to refer to recorded data from earlier lessons.

LESSON 5

Materials

For each student
- 1 science notebook
- 1 pencil with eraser

For each group of three students
- 1 design challenge card
- 1 standard vehicle
- 1 bucket of building pieces
- 1 large bookend with nonslip base, 23h × 15w × 20d cm (9h × 6w × 8d in), about 0.5 kg (1 lb)
- 1 string with paper clip hooks, wrapped around cardboard (from Lesson 4)
- 16 small washers in cup
- 3 large washers
- 2 blocks of wood, 5 × 8 × 9 cm (2 × 3 × 3½ in)
- 1 timer
- 1 circle template
- 1 metric ruler
- 1 set of colored pencils (to match building pieces)
- 1 strip of Masonite™, 38 × 122 × 0.6 cm (15 × 48 × ¼ in), or foamboard, 38 × 122 × 0.5 cm (15 × 48 × 3/16 in) (optional)

For the class
- 1 **Design Challenge Card: Lesson 5** (blackline master, pg. 70)
- 1 sheet of newsprint
- 1 measuring tape, 100 cm (39 in)
- Assorted colored markers
- Masking tape
- Extra string
- Jumbo paper clips
- Scissors
- Trade books on load-bearing vehicles

Preparation

1. Copy **Design Challenge Card: Lesson 5** (blackline master, pg. 70). Note that the blackline master contains two copies of the same challenge card. Cut each duplicated sheet into two cards. Each group needs one card.

2. Create two columns on the newsprint. Label the columns "What Made Our Vehicles Move Slowly" and "What Made Our Vehicles Move Fast." Date and hang the sheet.

3. Check each group's string with hooks. If a string is knotted, prepare a new one.

4. Arrange the materials at the distribution center.

5. Collect trade books that illustrate various load-bearing vehicles (such as trucks, minivans, moving vans, tractor trailers, wagons). Display the books for students to research various designs.

Procedure

1. Direct students' attention to the labeled newsprint. Ask students to write a few sentences in their notebooks about what caused their vehicles to move slowly and what caused them to move fast when they used the falling-weight system in Lessons 3 and 4.

2. Have students share their responses with the class. Using colored markers, record their ideas on the newsprint list in the appropriate columns. Sample student responses are shown in Figure 5-1. Ask students to brainstorm situations in which a vehicle would be required to move slowly or quickly.

Figure 5-1

Sample brainstorming list

3. Distribute one design challenge card to each group. Make certain students understand the requirements of the challenge. Discuss how they can apply the information collected in Lessons 3 and 4 to the challenge in this lesson.

4. Remind groups to give each member an opportunity to manipulate the building pieces and to help build the group's vehicle. Explain that once groups have met the challenge, they must be able to repeat their results for the teacher, another group, or the class. Ask students why repeatable results are important in science and engineering.

5. Ask groups to get their vehicles, trade books, and other materials and begin the design challenge. Students should set up their falling-weight systems just as they did in Lessons 3 and 4. They will also use a timer in this lesson.

Final Activities

1. Ask students to describe the process they used to build their vehicles and test the vehicles' motion. Use questions such as the following to guide the discussion:

   ■ **Designing and Planning:** Before building your vehicle, how did your group prepare?

   ■ **Building:** Did you experience any problems as you were building your vehicle? How did you solve them?

- **Testing:** How did you test your vehicle to determine whether it met the requirements? How did your vehicle move?
- **Evaluating:** Did you change anything about your vehicle or the falling-weight system after you tested it? What change did you make? Why did you make this change?

2. Have students use their pencils, colored pencils, circle templates, rulers, and graph paper to make a record (drawing) of their vehicles. (Students can use Figure 5-1 on pg. 25 of the Student Activity Book as a model.)

3. Ask students to clean up by doing the following:

- Remove the building pieces you added to your vehicles in this lesson. What should remain is the standard vehicle built in Lesson 2. You will use the standard vehicle again in Lesson 6. Students can refer to the technical drawing of the standard vehicle in Lesson 2 (pg. 36), if needed.
- Place any extra building pieces in your buckets.
- Return your standard vehicles and all other materials to the distribution center. Give the string and hooks to your teacher.
- Return the empty cardboard to the distribution center. You will use it in Lesson 9.

Management Tip: The following step can be completed now or at another time, such as during language arts.

4. Have students meet in pairs and read "Lunar Rover: Making Tracks on the Moon" (pgs. 68–69 in this guide and pgs. 26–27 in the Student Activity Book). As students read, ask them to think about why engineers designed this specialized vehicle to move slowly.

Extensions

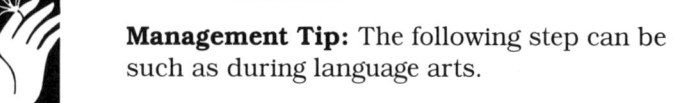

SOCIAL STUDIES   LANGUAGE ARTS

1. Have students survey adults to determine how many of them use design principles in their work. Students can also ask the interviewees in what ways they use design principles in their work. They can publish the interviews or a summary of their findings in a *Technological Design Newsletter* that they create. Encourage them to draw pictures or take photographs to include in the newsletter.

MATHEMATICS

2. Ask students to take repeated measurements of the time it takes their vehicles to move 60 cm (23½ in). Have students graph their data using a line plot (as in Lesson 4) or a line graph.

LANGUAGE ARTS   SOCIAL STUDIES

3. Have students research the airplane *Voyager*, which was the first plane designed to fly around the world without stopping to refuel. Ask them to answer the following questions. When did the *Voyager* make its first flight? How long did it take the plane to fly around the world? What design features of the plane helped save fuel?

SCIENCE   ART

4. Students can design and make their own paper airplanes. After a test flight, have students change the features of their paper airplanes to make them fly farther.

Assessment

In this lesson, students apply previously collected data and learned concepts and skills to the solution of their design challenge. As students build and test their vehicles, take notes on each student's progress. Use the following questions to help in your assessment.

Meeting the Design Challenge

- Does the student understand that the vehicle must meet a design requirement?
- Does the student understand what the requirement is?
- Does the student work cooperatively in the group in planning how to meet the design challenge? Does the group record its plan? (a sketch of the vehicle design, a written record of the number of washers)
- After building the vehicle, does the student work with the group to test it and evaluate its performance?
- If the vehicle does not initially meet the requirement, does the student work with the group to make a plan for improving the vehicle? Is the plan related to the test results?
- Does the student keep written records of test results?

Recording a Design

At the close of this lesson, you asked students to draw a representation of their vehicle. That drawing, together with the drawing from Lesson 2 and future lessons, can be used to assess improvement in each student's ability to record a design. Use the following questions to assist in the assessment:

- Does the student show improvement in his or her drawing ability?
- Does the student use a variety of techniques to make the drawings clear and easy to read? (color, labels, building pieces drawn in proportion) Did the student use these techniques in Lesson 2?
- Can the student effectively use drawing tools, such as a circle template, ruler, and colored pencils?
- Can the student draw the vehicle from one perspective? Or does the student combine several perspectives in one drawing?
- Does the student choose a perspective that clearly shows important features of the vehicle?
- Does the student create several drawings, each showing a different perspective?

Preparation for Lesson 6

At the end of this lesson, students should have removed from their vehicles all the pieces that are not part of the standard vehicle. They will need standard vehicles in Lesson 6.

LESSON 5

Reading Selection

Lunar Rover: Making Tracks on the Moon

Lunar Rover

Just imagine that you are an astronaut. Suppose you are flying a spacecraft to the Moon. Your goal is to learn about the Moon's surface. What kind of vehicle would you like to have there?

Engineers have already answered this question. In the Apollo space program, U.S. astronauts flew to the Moon. On many of these flights, the astronauts landed and walked on the Moon's surface. They took samples of Moon rocks and performed many scientific experiments. But since their oxygen supply was limited, they could only walk about 1 km (½ mile) away from their spacecraft. Many places they wanted to investigate were too far away.

To help the astronauts in their work on the moon, engineers designed a vehicle called the Lunar Rover. It was big enough to hold two astronauts, their equipment, and many samples of Moon rocks. What were the Lunar Rover's design requirements?

First of all, the Lunar Rover had to be light enough so that a rocket could lift it off Earth. The Rover weighed 210 kg (462 lb) on Earth. It only weighed 35 kg (77 lb) on the Moon. Do you know why?

How did the Lunar Rover get its energy to move? Most cars on Earth burn gasoline to drive their engines. Burning gasoline requires oxygen and oxygen comes from the air. Because there is no air on the Moon, a gasoline engine would not work. Instead, the Rover used electric motors, one for each wheel. Energy for the motors came from batteries.

The Rover had to move over the Moon's surface. Some of that surface is rough and uneven. The engineers made the tires big enough so that the Rover could roll over small bumps and cracks. To save on weight, engineers made these tires of wire. The tires looked like round metal cages, just like the cage around a small electric fan.

The Lunar Rover's top speed was about 12 km (7 miles) per hour. It needed to move slowly to save on the battery. The slow speed also helped astronauts control the vehicle on the rough terrain.

Engineers made careful records of their design for the Lunar Rover. They also recorded the results of all tests. Suppose engineers needed to build a vehicle to explore the surface of another planet, like Mars. What might this vehicle look like? Do some research and find out!

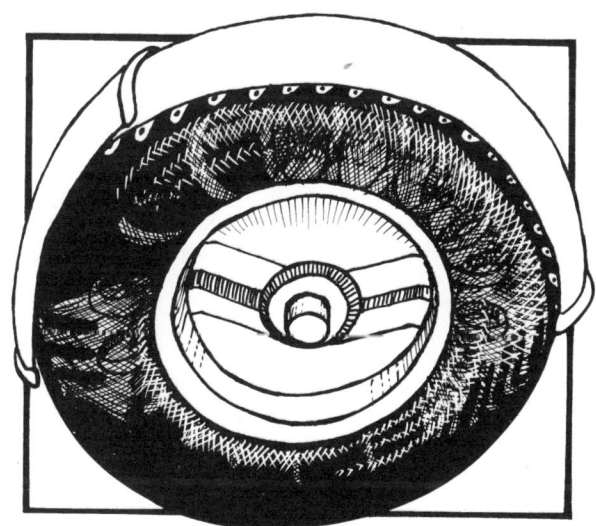

Close-up of Lunar Rover's tire

Blackline Master

Design Challenge Card: Lesson 5

Design Challenge

You are part of a famous engineering design team. Your team has been hired by "Out-of-This-World Vehicles," a company that specializes in designing space exploration vehicles. Your team must design and build a lunar vehicle that will move slowly on wheels across the lunar surface while being pulled by a rope. The design requirements are the following:

- Start with the standard vehicle. Add building pieces to make your design unique. Be creative.
- Your vehicle must be able to carry large lunar rocks (represented by blocks).
- Your vehicle must move across your work space in 4 to 6 seconds while being pulled by a rope.
- Deadline: You will have 30 minutes to complete the design challenge.

Good luck!

Design Challenge

You are part of a famous engineering design team. Your team has been hired by "Out-of-This-World Vehicles," a company that specializes in designing space exploration vehicles. Your team must design and build a lunar vehicle that will move slowly on wheels across the lunar surface while being pulled by a rope. The design requirements are the following:

- Start with the standard vehicle. Add building pieces to make your design unique. Be creative.
- Your vehicle must be able to carry large lunar rocks (represented by blocks).
- Your vehicle must move across your work space in 4 to 6 seconds while being pulled by a rope.
- Deadline: You will have 30 minutes to complete the design challenge.

Good luck!

STC / *Motion and Design*

LESSON 6

Evaluating Vehicle Design: Looking at Rubber Band Energy

Overview and Objectives

Earlier, students explored the motion of their vehicles when pulled by a weighted string. Now they are ready to explore another way of moving their vehicles—by releasing the energy stored in a stretched rubber band and using it to turn an axle. To prepare for this exploration of "rubber band energy," students evaluate the standard vehicles they used in previous lessons and test various ways the rubber band can be used to move them. This investigation prepares students for Lesson 7, in which they conduct a formal investigation of the distance traveled by their axle-driven vehicles.

- Students attempt to move their vehicles using rubber band energy.
- Students evaluate the design of their standard vehicles for rubber band energy.
- Students discuss the results of their evaluations.

Background

Energy, or the capacity for doing work, is a basic concept in physical science. Many sources of energy in nature are familiar to students. The sun's energy warms the earth and enables plants to grow. Wood and coal provide chemical energy that can be used for heating homes and businesses. Wind energy can turn windmills and move sailboats. Students may already have an intuitive understanding of stored energy. Our bodies use the energy stored in food, a flashlight uses the energy stored in its batteries, and a car uses the energy stored in gasoline.

Energy exists in many forms. **Stored energy, or potential energy,** is energy ready to be released. In Lesson 3, students stored energy in the weight on the string when they raised it from the floor to the height of the work space. When students released the weight, gravity pulled it to the ground and the string pulled the vehicle along the work space. As the weight descended, its stored energy was converted to the energy of motion of both the weight and the vehicle. Physicists call the energy of motion **kinetic energy.**

In this lesson, students evaluate the effectiveness of their vehicles' design when it is driven by the energy stored in a stretched rubber band. If you hold the ends of a rubber band and pull your hands slowly apart, the rubber band lengthens, but you can also feel it pulling your hands back in. When students wind the rubber band around the axle of their vehicles, they store energy in the rubber band.

When stored energy is released, it changes form. For example, when an archer pulls back on a bowstring, the bow bends and the string stretches. The archer has stored energy in the bow and string. When the archer releases the arrow, the stored energy

STC / *Motion and Design*

LESSON 6

is transformed into the motion of the arrow. Likewise, the wound-up rubber band on the vehicle's axle has stored energy. When students release their vehicle, the rubber band unwinds and the stored energy is converted to the vehicle's energy of motion.

During a free exploration period, students observe how their vehicles can move with rubber band energy. Then in a structured exploration, they attach one end of a rubber band to the vehicle's fixed axle and wind the other end around the free-spinning axle. As students turn the free axle to wind the rubber band around it, the amount of energy stored in the rubber band increases. When students release the axle, the stored energy causes the axle and the attached wheels to spin and the vehicle to move.

During this observation, students may notice one or more of the following: the tires grip the work surface and help the vehicle move, the tan hub connectors lock the large wheels to the axle, and the crossbar prevents the frame from moving. Lesson 8 provides a more detailed exploration of these design features as they relate to friction. Evaluating such design features in greater detail will help prepare students for building their own vehicles later in the unit.

Materials

For each student
- 1 science notebook
- 1 pencil with eraser
- Safety goggles

For each group of three students
- 1 copy of **Record Sheet 6-A: Evaluating Our Vehicle Design for Rubber Band Energy**
- 1 standard vehicle
- 3 No. 16 rubber bands, connected

Preparation

1. Make one copy of **Record Sheet 6-A: Evaluating Our Vehicle Design for Rubber Band Energy** for each group (or student).

2. For each group, connect three rubber bands. Use Figure 6-1 as your guide.

Figure 6-1

Connecting the rubber bands

3. Identify an area on the floor for students to work, since many of the vehicles may travel farther than the length of a work space.

4. Check to make certain that each group removed any extra pieces from their vehicle at the end of Lesson 5 and restored it to the standard vehicle (as built in Lesson 2, see pg. 36). If any groups do not have a standard vehicle, ask them to build it.

5. Arrange the vehicles and rubber bands at the distribution center.

LESSON 6

Procedure

1. Distribute a pair of safety goggles to each student. Review the reasons and proper procedures for wearing them. Remind students that for safety reasons, they should wear the goggles any time they are using rubber bands with their vehicles.

Figure 6-2

Wearing safety goggles

2. Ask each group to collect their standard vehicle and set of connected rubber bands from the distribution center. Allow about five to seven minutes for students to explore freely how they might use the connected rubber bands to move their vehicles.

3. After all groups have explored how rubber bands might be used to move their vehicles, ask if any group was able to move its vehicle with rubber band energy. If so, have the group demonstrate. Ask students to describe which vehicle design features might have helped their vehicles move with rubber band energy.

4. Distribute one copy of **Record Sheet 6-A: Evaluating Our Vehicle Design for Rubber Band Energy** to each group (or student). Review the instructions. Point out the area on the floor that you have identified for students to further explore rubber band energy.

5. Ask students to carry out the investigation and complete the record sheet.

Final Activities

1. Ask students to refer to their record sheets as they share what they discovered about rubber band energy. Include in the discussion such issues as the following:

   ■ What did you feel in your hand as you wound the rubber band? Did this feeling change as you wound the rubber band tighter? If so, how?

   ■ Did the direction in which you wound the rubber band affect the direction in which your vehicle traveled? If so, how?

2. Discuss students' initial observations of how the rubber band affected the distance their vehicles traveled. What did they do to make their vehicles move a longer distance? What did they do to make their vehicles move a shorter distance? Do they know why this happened? Let students know they will conduct a formal investigation of this phenomenon in Lesson 7.

LESSON 6

3. Ask students to return their standard vehicles and other materials to the distribution center. Make certain each vehicle is in its standard configuration. Students can refer to the technical drawing in Lesson 2 (pg. 36), if needed.

Extensions

ART | **LANGUAGE ARTS**

1. Ask students to bring in advertisements for automobiles and trucks. Have them prepare their own advertisement promoting the special features of one of these vehicles. Their advertisement could take the form of a skit or a poster board display.

SOCIAL STUDIES

2. Have students conduct research to find out how the design of the automobile has changed over time. Ask students to create a time line to show these changes. Students might also research changes in other inventions, such as the telephone or computer.

SCIENCE | **SOCIAL STUDIES**

3. Ask students to bring in an item from home—for example, clothing, kitchenware, shop tools, writing implements, or sports equipment—and discuss how the item's function determined its design.

Preparation for Lesson 7

- Students will use their standard vehicles in Lesson 7. Remind them not to modify or disassemble their vehicles between lessons.

- Students will need a large floor area to test the motion of their vehicles in Lesson 7. You can push the desks to the sides of your classroom. Or you may want to reserve a resource room, cafeteria, or gym.

Record Sheet 6–A   Names: _____

Date: _____

Evaluating Our Vehicle Design for Rubber Band Energy

1. As shown in the illustration, attach the connected rubber bands to the axle (the red rod) near the small wheels by looping it around the axle.

2. Stretch the loose end of the rubber band to the other axle, near the large wheels. Wind the loose end several times around this axle. (The illustrations on the next page of this record sheet will help you.) Let go of the rubber band. What happened? Why do you think this happened?

_____

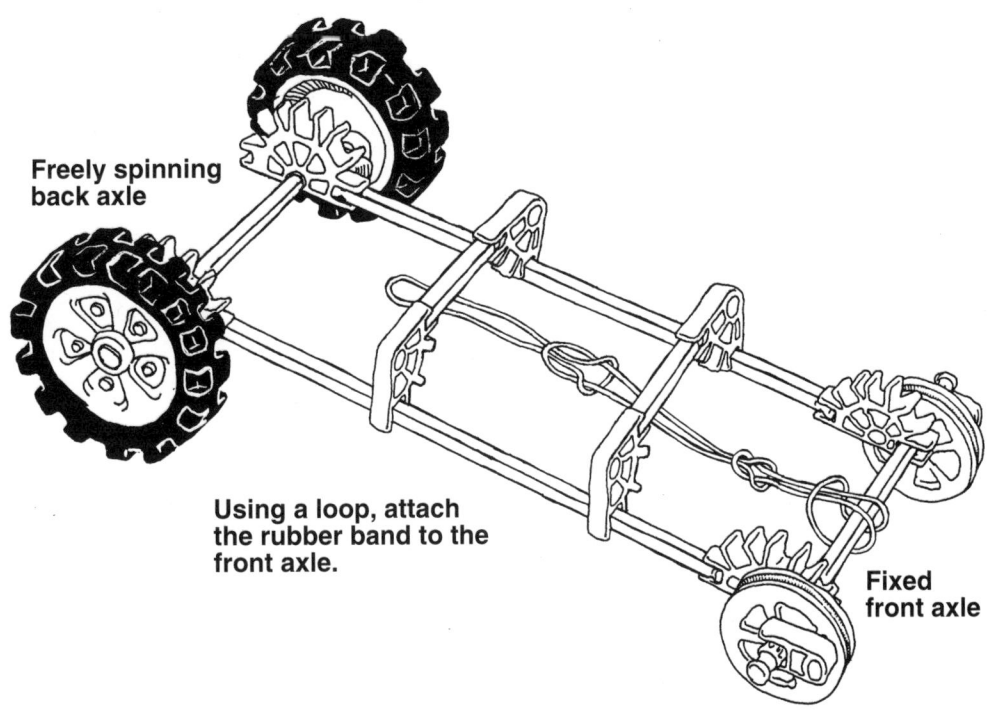

Freely spinning back axle

Using a loop, attach the rubber band to the front axle.

Fixed front axle

3. Explore other ways of using the rubber band to move your vehicle.
   - Wind the rubber band in opposite directions—over the axle and then under the axle. What do you observe each time?

   _____

   _____

   - Remove the rubber band. Attach one end of it to the axle that spins. Then wind the other end around the fixed axle. Let go. What do you observe?

   _____

   _____

STC / *Motion and Design*

LESSON 6

Record Sheet 6–A   Names: _____

_____

_____

Evaluating Our Vehicle Design for Rubber Band Energy, *continued*

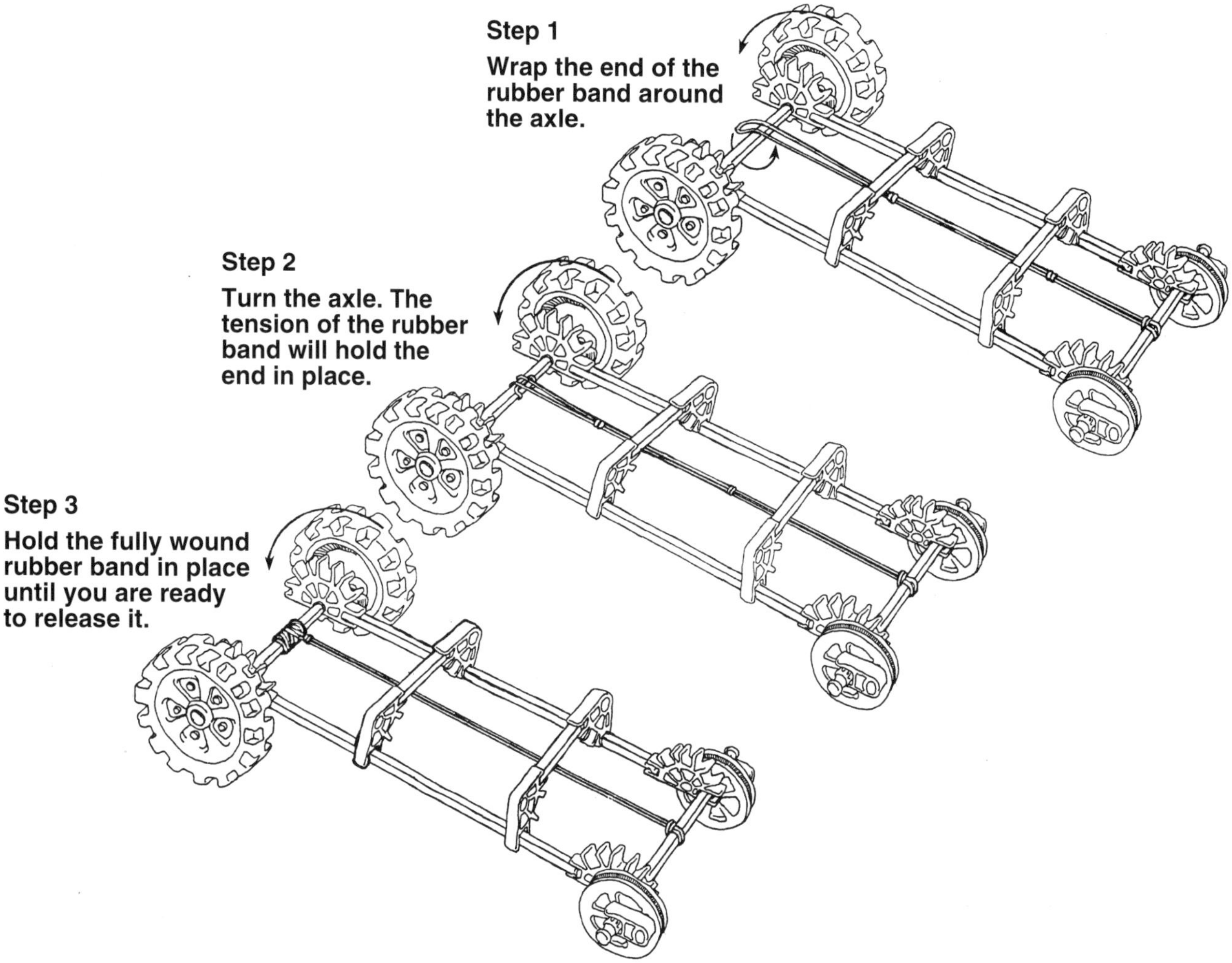

Step 1
Wrap the end of the rubber band around the axle.

Step 2
Turn the axle. The tension of the rubber band will hold the end in place.

Step 3
Hold the fully wound rubber band in place until you are ready to release it.

4. What other observations have you made about your axle-driven vehicle and how it moves with rubber band energy?

_____

_____

_____

STC / *Motion and Design*

LESSON 7

Testing the Effects of Rubber Band Energy

Overview and Objectives

In Lesson 6, students evaluated the features of their standard vehicles to determine if they could move with rubber band energy. In this lesson, they record the number of times they wind a rubber band around an axle and observe how this variable affects the distance their vehicles travel. Students make predictions and collect data before reporting their results to the class. Groups compare and identify patterns in their results. Discussion of these patterns helps students appreciate the concept of stored energy. This information enhances students' understanding of the variables that affect the speed and distance their axle-driven vehicle can move. It also prepares them for upcoming investigations in which they study the effects of friction on the motion of their vehicles.

- Students predict and investigate how variations in rubber band energy affect the distance their vehicles travel.
- Students record their results.
- Students share results and identify patterns.
- Students discuss the relationship between the number of turns of the rubber band around the axle and the distance their axle-driven vehicles travel.

Background

In Lesson 6, students discovered that the rubber band stretches when they wind it around the axle of their vehicles. The rubber band has the potential to move the vehicle because of its stored energy. However, there is no motion until students release the wound rubber band.

As the number of turns on the rubber band increases, so does the energy stored in the rubber band. As the stored energy increases, so does the initial speed acquired by the axle-driven vehicle and the distance it can travel. The faster the vehicle moves, the more energy of motion it has.

When the rubber band is completely unwound, it has no more energy to give the vehicle. However, the vehicle continues to roll while friction slows it down. Friction opposes the vehicle's forward motion as it changes the energy of motion into the energy of heat. (Friction also acts on the vehicle while it speeds up, but the rubber band force overwhelms friction during this part of the motion.) Students can see this relationship between stored energy and energy of motion when they use self-stick dots to record the distances their axle-driven vehicles travel with each number of turns on the rubber band.

STC / Motion and Design

LESSON 7

Although students will be using two, four, and eight turns of the rubber band in this investigation (each trial doubling the previous trial's number of turns), there is not a directly proportional relationship between the number of turns and the distance the vehicle travels. In other words, four turns on the rubber band does not make the vehicle move twice as far as two turns. It moves even farther. If students complete the mathematics extension in this lesson, in which they record the measurements for each distance traveled, they may find this out. Ask students how the eighth turn on the rubber band "feels" in relation to the first turn. Most will report that it was "tighter"—there was more "tension"—when they turned the rubber band the eighth time. This finding is evidence that each turn stores more energy per turn than the last.

Materials

For each student
- 1 science notebook
- 1 pencil with eraser
- Safety goggles

For each group of three students
- 1 standard vehicle
- 3 No. 16 rubber bands, connected
- 1 strip of adding machine tape, 4 m (13 ft)
- 3 self-stick red dots, 2 cm (¾ in)
- 3 self-stick blue dots, 2 cm (¾ in)
- 3 self-stick green dots, 2 cm (¾ in)

For the class
- Masking tape
- Adding machine tape

Preparation

1. Students' vehicles may move up to 4 m or more in this lesson. Prepare an area of your room where they can test and measure the distances their vehicles travel. Or if you have access to a gym or cafeteria, reserve it ahead of time. (Students will get good results on carpeted surfaces; however, their vehicles may travel farther on hardwood or vinyl.)

2. Cut the adding machine tape into strips that measure 4 m (13 ft) long. Each group starts with one strip. Prepare extra strips for groups whose vehicles travel more than 4 m.

3. Arrange the vehicles and materials at the distribution center.

4. Make certain all vehicles are in their standard configuration. Students can refer to the technical drawing in Lesson 2 (pg. 36), if needed.

Procedure

1. Let students know they will make predictions and collect data to investigate how the number of turns of the rubber band on the axle affects the distance their vehicles travel. Have students record in their notebooks a prediction about this relationship. Discuss their predictions.

2. Review with students the **Student Instructions for Collecting Data on Rubber Band Energy** (pgs. 86–87 in this guide and pgs. 34–35 in the Student Activity Book). Use the illustrations on the instruction sheet to

establish starting and stopping points on the paper strip. (For example, students might decide as a class that the front wheels of the vehicles must be behind or on the starting line before they can release the vehicles. When measuring the stopping point of a vehicle in each trial, students might decide that they want to put the self-stick dots on the paper strip near the position of the front wheels and not the back ones.) The student instructions suggest one method. This will ensure that comparisons among groups are fair. Discuss with your students why these procedures are important.

3. Have students pick up their vehicles and other materials from the distribution center and conduct the investigation.

4. Ask students to return their vehicles and materials to the distribution center. Remind students not to disassemble their vehicles.

Final Activities

1. Invite groups to display their paper strips. You may wish to tape the strips horizontally, one above the other, on the chalkboard, a wall, or the floor. Ask students to discuss what differences and patterns they observe among the vehicles at each number of turns of the rubber band around the axle. Have groups point out the predicted stopping point for their axle-driven vehicles and compare each prediction to the actual distance. How did their results compare with their predictions?

Figure 7-1

Evaluating our results

Management Tip: The discussion in the next step asks students to focus on the energy stored in and released from the rubber band. The prompts are provided to help you guide the discussion; students' answers may vary, which is fine. Remember that students at this level often have an intuitive understanding of why the rubber band can be used to move their vehicles, but the goal of this discussion is to help them *verbalize* their ideas about energy being stored in the rubber band.

2. Encourage students to think about their rubber bands in terms of stored energy and transfer of energy by asking them questions such as the following:

- Where does the energy to wind the rubber band come from? (your muscles, fueled by sugar in your blood)

LESSON 7

- Where does the energy to move the vehicle come from? (rubber band)
- How do you store energy in the rubber band? (wind rubber band around axle)
- How do you release the energy stored in the rubber band? (let go of vehicle)
- What happens when the stored energy in the rubber band is released? (vehicle gains energy of motion, axle turns)
- How does the number of turns on the rubber band affect the distance the vehicle travels? (more energy stored means farther distance)
- Why was it important to keep the number of turns the same for all groups in the class? (to make fair comparisons)
- What would happen if the number of turns was only 1? What if the number of turns was 10?

3. Let students know that in Lessons 8 and 9 they will evaluate specific design features of their axle-driven vehicles to determine what helps them move and what slows their motion.

Figure 7-2

Marking the distances traveled

Extensions

MATHEMATICS

1. Have groups use the 100-cm (39-in) tapes to measure the distances their vehicle travels when the rubber band is turned around the axle two, four, and eight times. Students can measure the distance from the starting line to each dot on their strip of paper and record the distances (in cm) on a data table like the one shown in Figure 7-3. Then they can select the dot that best represents all of the distances the vehicle travels. This measurement might be the distance of the middle dot, the distance where the dots cluster, or the greatest distance.

LESSON 7

Figure 7-3

Sample data table

Number of Turns of the Rubber Band	Distance Traveled (in cm)			Selected Distance
	Trial 1	Trial 2	Trial 3	
2				
4				
8				

MATHEMATICS

2. Ask students who completed Extension 1 in this lesson to graph their selected distances.

SCIENCE

3. Take students to the lunchroom, gym, or another room that has a smooth, hard floor. Have groups set up their vehicles along one wall. Challenge groups to hold a race and make their vehicles go as far as possible.

SCIENCE

4. Have students use masking tape to mark off both sides of a "dogleg" race track. (A dogleg is something having an abrupt angle like a dog's leg.) Students can race their axle-driven vehicles on each leg of the track. The vehicles must remain inside the racing lane. Before they race, have them predict, for each leg, how many turns of the rubber band are needed to move their vehicles the given distance.

SCIENCE

5. Challenge students to investigate what happens if they add a load (wooden blocks) to their axle-driven vehicles. Also ask them to find out how the position of the load affects the way their vehicles move.

Preparation for Lesson 8

Students will use their standard vehicles in Lesson 8.

Student Instructions for Collecting Data on Rubber Band Energy

1. You will need an area of the floor where your vehicle can move a long distance—anywhere from 1 m (39 in) to 10 m (33 ft).

2. Roll out your strip of paper. Tape it to the floor.

3. Make a starting line with masking tape at one end of the strip of paper.

4. Wind your connected rubber bands two times around the axle that holds the large wheels. Put the vehicle's front wheels on the starting line. Before you let go of the vehicle, have your group make a prediction. Use a pencil to mark on the paper the distance you think your vehicle will travel.

5. Let go of your vehicle. Observe what happens.

6. Put a **red** dot on the paper strip where the front wheels of your vehicle stop.

7. Repeat the test two more times:

    - Wind the rubber band the same number of times (two) for each trial.
    - Use a pencil to mark a prediction each time.
    - Let go of the vehicle.
    - How far did your vehicle move? Mark the stopping point with a red dot.

8. Once you have three red dots on your paper, look at the dots. What do you notice about their positions? Record your observations in your notebook.

9. Which dot represents the distance your vehicle traveled most often? Circle that dot with a pencil.

10. Now wind your rubber band four times around the axle. Then do the following:

    - Predict how far you think your vehicle will travel when the rubber band is wound four times. Use a pencil to mark your prediction on the paper strip.
    - Test how far your vehicle travels with four turns on the rubber band.
    - Put a **blue** dot on your paper strip to mark the distance.
    - Do this three times altogether, winding the band four times and marking a prediction each time.

11. Look at the blue dots. What do you observe about all the distances your vehicle traveled? How close was your prediction to the actual distances your vehicle traveled? Record your observations in your notebook.

12. Which dot do you think best represents all the distances your vehicle moved? Use a pencil to circle that dot.

13. Now wind the rubber band eight times around the axle. How does it feel to wind the rubber band eight times compared with two? Discuss this with your group.

14. With the rubber band wound eight times around the axle, repeat the test as follows:

    - Record your prediction on the strip of paper. How far do you think the vehicle will move?
    - Let go of the vehicle. Use **green** dots to mark the distance.
    - Test the vehicle three times altogether.
    - Circle the dot that best represents all the distances your vehicle traveled.
    - Record your observations in your notebook.

| LESSON 8 | **Evaluating Vehicle Design: Looking at Friction** |

Overview and Objectives

In Lessons 6 and 7, students explored and then tested ways in which they could use the energy stored in a stretched rubber band to move an axle-driven vehicle. In this lesson, they examine specific design features of their vehicles propelled by a rubber band and focus on how these features create friction that opposes or enhances the vehicles' motion. By identifying the relationship between surfaces rubbing together and the vehicles' motion, students begin to appreciate how friction affects performance and why engineers must consider it when they design vehicles or any device with moving parts. This knowledge prepares students for upcoming lessons in which they design their own axle-driven vehicles and investigate the effects of air friction on the vehicles' motion.

- Students brainstorm what they know and what they want to know about friction.

- Students evaluate specific design features that reduce or increase friction on vehicles propelled by a rubber band.

- Students share their observations of vehicle design features and the role of friction in vehicular motion.

Background

Pulling or pushing forces are always involved when a vehicle—or any object—speeds up, slows down, or changes its direction. Some vehicles also experience considerable friction, which is a force that opposes motion. The friction between the vehicle's wheels and the axle slows the vehicle's forward motion. Similarly, when a wagon rolls on a level sidewalk, the force of friction between the turning axles and the frame of the wagon eventually slows the wagon to a halt, unless something exerts an additional force by pulling or pushing it.

What happens to the energy of motion as friction slows a vehicle? Think of pulling on a rope, having it slip through your hands, and getting a rope burn. The friction between your hands and the slipping rope produces heat. In the same way, the brakes of a car produce heat as the brake pads rub against the brake drums or the disks. Throughout this unit, students' vehicles will slow to a stop. Wheels rub against axles. Axles rub against the connectors that support them. All this rubbing produces friction. Some of the energy of motion is lost as a small amount of heat—an amount too small for students to observe—while the vehicles slow down.

In this lesson, students look at three vehicle design features that can create friction and influence a vehicle's motion: the wheels and tan hub connectors, the frame, and the tires. Some design features reduce friction between vehicle parts. For example, the wheels of some small vehicles have a little bulge on both sides

LESSON 8

of the central part of the wheel, or **hub.** This bulge sets the wheel out from the frame that supports the axle and reduces frictional contact. It confines any rubbing between the wheel and the frame to the hub. The wheels in the students' building set have no such bulge. To reduce wheel friction, the standard vehicle contains tan hub connectors between the large wheels and the frame. The tan hub connectors not only fix the wheels to the turning axle so the wheels will spin with the axle and move the vehicle, but they also ensure that any friction between the wheels and the frame occurs at the connector, which is close enough to the axle to minimize the effects of friction.

Students may already have observed that the crossbars strengthen the frame of their vehicles. If the crossbars are removed and the frame bends, the wheels and axles might rub on the frame. The resulting friction would oppose the vehicles' motion.

This friction between the wheels and axle and the wheels and frame is termed "wasteful" friction in this unit because it reduces, or "wastes," the energy needed for motion. In contrast, friction that helps a vehicle to move can be considered "useful." For instance, tires must grip the road so a vehicle can change speed or turn. If you imagine a race car on ice, you will realize how useful friction is. Friction also helps people move. The friction between the soles of our shoes and the ground allows us to walk. Without useful friction, we would simply shuffle in place, rather than move forward. When students remove the rubber tires from their vehicles in this lesson, they may observe that the wheels "spin out" when rubber band energy is applied. Without the useful friction created when the tires and the surface rub together, the vehicle could not move forward.

Materials

For each student
1 science notebook
1 pencil with eraser
  Safety goggles

For each group of three students
1 copy of **Record Sheet 8-A: Evaluating Vehicle Design for Friction**
1 standard vehicle with connected rubber bands
1 timer

For the class
1 sheet of newsprint
  Assorted colored markers
  Masking tape

Preparation

1. Make one copy of **Record Sheet 8-A: Evaluating Vehicle Design for Friction** for each group.

2. Label the sheet of newsprint "What We Know and Want to Find Out about Friction." Date and hang the sheet.

3. Arrange the materials at the distribution center. Make certain the rubber bands are connected in sets of three and attached to the vehicles.

Procedure

1. Have each group collect its standard vehicle from the distribution center. Ask students to turn their vehicle on its side, hold it up and away from the table, hold the gray bar, and with one hand spin the large wheel. Have the class discuss what they observe. Focus the discussion by asking students what they think causes the wheel to slow down and eventually stop moving.

Figure 8-1

Turning the vehicle on its side

2. Brainstorm as a class what students already know about friction and what questions they would like answered. Record their responses on the brainstorming list.

3. Have students rub their hands together. What happens? Encourage students to discuss events in their daily lives that involve friction. Let students know they will evaluate the design of their vehicles to determine the various effects friction has on their motion.

4. Distribute **Record Sheet 8-A: Evaluating Vehicle Design for Friction.** Each group will have three observation cards. Review the questions on each observation card with the class. Let students know they are to record as many observations about each design feature as possible. The questions on the cards are only suggestions and should not limit their observations. Students should try to complete as many observation cards as possible in the lesson.

5. Have each group pick up the safety goggles for each group member and a timer. Then ask groups to begin their evaluation.

Management Tips

- You may want to ask groups to return their timer to the distribution center once they have completed card one. This way, the timer will not become a distraction.

- Students can complete cards one (wheels) and two (tires) at their desks. However, when completing card three (frame), they will need a large floor space to test their vehicles' motion.

LESSON 8

Final Activities

1. When students have completed their evaluations, ask a member from each group to share what the group observed about each vehicle design feature. Encourage the other groups to ask questions or elaborate as needed.

2. Discuss vehicle design features that can either increase or decrease friction using questions such as the following:

   - Is there anything on your vehicle that rubs together? (tires against the frame, wheels against the axle)
   - What can this rubbing do to the motion of your vehicle? (slows it down, takes away energy available to vehicle, creates wasteful friction)
   - What vehicle design features help reduce the amount of rubbing between the wheels and the vehicle's axle and frame? (tan hub connectors, crossbars)
   - What vehicle design features increase the friction between the floor or work surface and the wheels? (tires)
   - How does this rubbing influence your vehicle's motion? (creates useful friction, helps it move)

3. Let students know they can use the information they learned in this lesson when they build vehicles in upcoming lessons.

4. Ask students to return their materials to the distribution center. Remind them not to disassemble their standard vehicles; they will add to them in Lesson 9.

Extensions

SCIENCE

1. Challenge students to design investigations that demonstrate useful and wasteful friction. One test of useful friction might be the following. Have students place plastic bags over their shoes and then walk across a carpeted surface. Have them remove the bags and walk again. They can compare the two trials. Which way made walking easier? Why? Have students describe the friction between their shoes and the carpet. Then have them make a list of other situations in their lives that involve useful and wasteful friction.

SOCIAL STUDIES   LANGUAGE ARTS

2. Ask students to research a technological invention, from any period in history, in which friction was a design consideration. Examples include the bicycle, swing set, skis, and roller skates.

SCIENCE   LANGUAGE ARTS

3. Have students research and report on how friction affects objects entering the earth's atmosphere. Examples include the space shuttle coming in for a landing or a meteor approaching earth. Why does the space shuttle need a heat shield? How does the meteor's shape change and why?

SCIENCE

4. Students can perform tests of friction by dragging weights behind their moving vehicles. How does this influence the vehicles' motion? Why?

Preparation for Lesson 9

Students will use their standard vehicles in Lesson 9.

LESSON 8

Record Sheet 8–A   Names: _____

Date: _____

Evaluating Vehicle Design for Friction

Observation Card One

Design Feature: Wheels and Tan Hub Connectors

Observations

_____
_____
_____
_____
_____
_____
_____

Ideas for observations: What is the job of the tan hub connector? Turn the vehicle on its side and hold the gray rod. Spin the large wheel. Time how long it spins. Do this several times. Now remove the large wheel and its tan hub connector. Turn the wheel over. Put it back on the axle so the small hole on the wheel faces out. Put the tan hub connector on the *outside* of the wheel. (Connect it to the small hole of the wheel.) Now spin the wheel again. Time its spin. What do you observe? How did the wheel spin differently each time? Why do you think this happened? (Remember to return the tan hub connector to the *inside* of the wheel when you are finished.)

STC / *Motion and Design*

LESSON 8

Record Sheet 8–A

Names: _____

_____

_____

Evaluating Vehicle Design for Friction, *continued*

Observation Card Two

Design Feature: Tires

Observations

_____

_____

_____

_____

_____

_____

Ideas for observations: Remove the black tires from the large wheels. Use the rubber band to move the vehicle without its tires. What do you observe? What do you think is the job of the tires? (Remember to put the tires on again when you are finished.)

STC / *Motion and Design*

LESSON 8

Record Sheet 8–A   Names: _____

_____

_____

Evaluating Vehicle Design for Friction, *continued*

Observation Card Three

Design Feature: Frame and Crossbars

Observations

_____
_____
_____
_____
_____
_____

Ideas for observations: Remove the two blue crossbars. Squeeze the frame gently. Then pull the gray bars out gently. Now try to use the rubber band to move the vehicle. What changes do you observe when you remove the crossbars? What do you think is the job of the crossbars? How can the frame without the crossbars affect the spinning wheels? (Remember to put the crossbars on again when you are finished.)

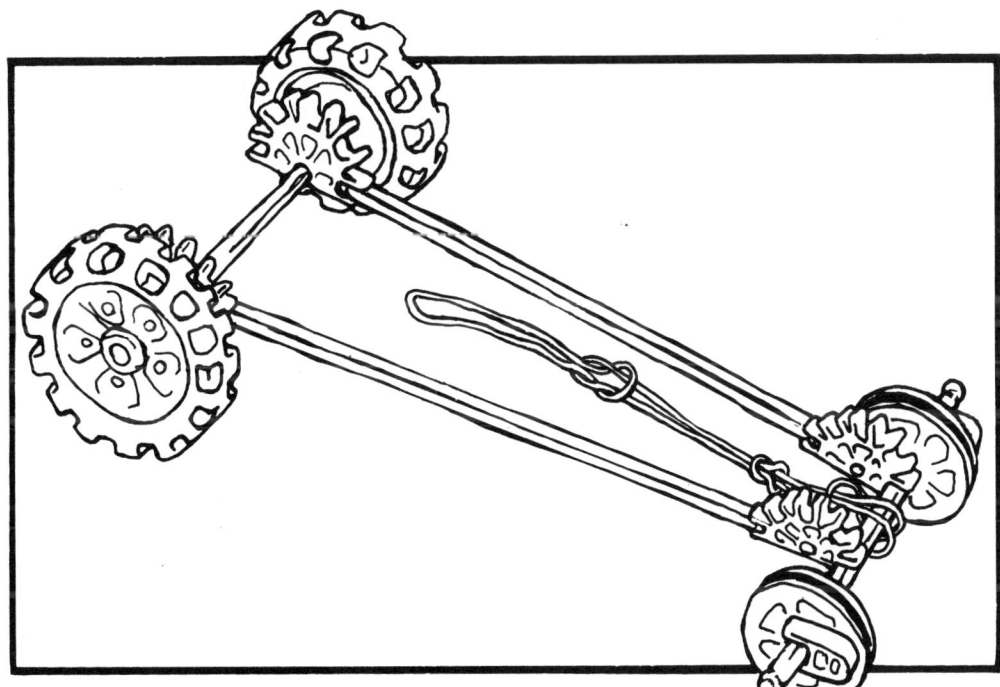

STC / *Motion and Design*

LESSON 9

Designing and Building a Vehicle with a Sail

Overview and Objectives

Having examined the ways in which friction affects the motion of an axle-driven vehicle, students are ready to apply their knowledge of friction to a new situation—studying the effects of air resistance on a vehicle's motion. To prepare for this study, each group uses design process skills to modify its axle-driven vehicle to hold a sail. By discussing their initial observations, students prepare for Lesson 10, in which they conduct a formal investigation to test how air pushing against the sail affects their vehicles' motion.

- Students brainstorm how a sail might affect the motion of their axle-driven vehicles.
- Students adapt their vehicles to hold a cardboard sail.
- Students make initial observations about the influence of the sail on the vehicles' motion and discuss these observations.
- Students reflect on their work by completing a self-assessment.

Background

In this lesson, students modify their axle-driven vehicles by adding a cardboard sail. Because there is no best solution to this new design challenge, the lesson encourages diverse approaches and outcomes. Students can learn from each other while they work in their own groups and watch others. It is important to emphasize that an essential part of the design process is evaluating and refining the product. Like engineers, students must repeatedly refine their vehicles, test them, and record results to keep track of the effects of each new change.

In brainstorming how a sail might affect a vehicle's motion, it is important to review the ways in which students moved their vehicles both faster and slower in earlier lessons. To make their vehicles go faster, students may have done the following:

- Increased the force when pulling the vehicle with a weighted string by increasing the number of washers (Lesson 3).
- Decreased the resistance to motion by reducing the vehicle's load (Lesson 4).
- Increased the amount of energy stored in the vehicle by increasing the number of turns of the rubber band around the axle (Lesson 7).
- Minimized friction by placing tan hub connectors and crossbars on their vehicle to reduce the rubbing of wheels on the frame (Lesson 8).

LESSON 9

To make their vehicles go slower, students may have done the following:

- Decreased the force when pulling the vehicle with the weighted string by decreasing the number of washers (Lesson 3).

- Increased the resistance to motion by increasing the vehicle's load with additional building pieces or blocks of wood (Lessons 4 and 5).

- Decreased the amount of energy stored in the vehicle by decreasing the number of turns of the rubber band around the axle (Lesson 7).

- Increased friction by removing the tan hub connectors between the axles, frame, and wheels (Lesson 8).

Most students' familiarity with sails will focus on sailboats, in which a sail catches the wind and moves the boat. A sail, however, can also slow a vehicle down. When the wind is too strong or blowing in the wrong direction, a sailor will furl, or fold, the sail, so the wind does not push against the sail. When students add a cardboard sail to their vehicles in this lesson, they will probably make preliminary observations about the sail and its effect on the vehicles' motion. They might notice that their vehicle does not move as far as it did in Lesson 7.

In this lesson, students complete a self-assessment. Do not grade it. Its purpose is to help you assess each student's attitudes about the unit and evaluate how each group is working so you can consider regrouping if necessary. It will also help you identify students' concerns and misconceptions so that you can address them before the unit's end.

Materials

For each student
- 1 science notebook
- 1 copy of **Student Self-Assessment A**
- Safety goggles

For each group of three students
- 1 standard vehicle
- 1 bucket of building pieces
- 1 piece of cardboard, 23 × 30 cm (9 × 12 in)
- 3 No. 16 rubber bands, connected
- 1 set of colored pencils
- 1 metric ruler
- 1 circle template

For the class
- Brainstorming list, "What Made Our Vehicles Move Slowly and What Made Our Vehicles Move Fast" (from Lesson 5)
- Assorted colored markers
- Masking tape
- 2 single-hole punches (optional)
- Trade books or advertisements that show vehicles with sails

Preparation

1. Make a copy of **Student Self-Assessment A** for each student.

2. Check the connected rubber bands. If they have become less elastic, replace them.

LESSON 9

3. Display the brainstorming list from Lesson 5. Set out the colored markers.

4. Collect trade books or advertisements that show vehicles with sails. Display the trade books for students to use when designing their vehicles or to look at in their spare time.

5. Check the vehicles to make certain they are in their standard form. If some are not, have a member from each group modify its vehicle before beginning the lesson (see Lesson 2, pg. 36).

6. Arrange the vehicles and materials at the distribution center. You may want to set out one or more single-hole punches and rolls of masking tape for groups that have difficulty attaching the sail. Or cut a 30-cm (12-in) strip of masking tape for each group and hang the strips along one end of the distribution table.

Procedure

1. Direct students' attention to the brainstorming list from Lesson 5. Encourage them to suggest any new ideas they have about what might cause their vehicles to move slowly or fast. Use a marker of a different color to add their new ideas to the list.

2. Have students hypothesize what influences a sail might have if it were fastened to their vehicles. Use another colored marker to add these ideas to the brainstorming list. (If students do not mention it, encourage them to discuss how the sail might affect the vehicle's motion when moving *with* the wind and *against* it. Also ask students if the sail would have any effect on the motion of the vehicle if there were no wind.)

3. Let students know they will adapt their standard vehicles to hold an upright piece of cardboard—like a sail—that will catch the air. Students may want to sketch their designs in their notebooks before building and use the trade books to research possible designs. They should use the entire piece of cardboard. Two sample vehicles are shown in Figure 9-1.

4. After students discuss their plans with the group, have each group get its bucket of building pieces, vehicle, connected rubber bands, and piece of cardboard. After students attach the cardboard sail to their standard vehicles, ask them to return the buckets to the distribution center.

Management Tip: Some groups may have difficulty attaching the cardboard sail in an upright position to their vehicle. If they request assistance, suggest that they use masking tape or punch two or three holes in the sail. Students can insert rods through the holes, which will facilitate fastening the sail. Make these suggestions only if groups have attempted their own design and have not succeeded.

Final Activities

1. Ask students to discuss how they completed the design challenge. What successes did they have? What problems did they encounter? How did they solve them?

2. Ask students to **hypothesize,** or make an educated guess about, how the sail might affect the vehicle's motion when the sail is pushing against the air. Let students know they will test their hypotheses in Lesson 10.

3. Have students clean up by carefully placing their vehicles with the attached sail on the distribution center. Students can label their vehicles with tape.

Management Tip: Students can complete the following steps now or at another more convenient time before Lesson 11.

LESSON 9

Figure 9-1

Sample student vehicles with a sail

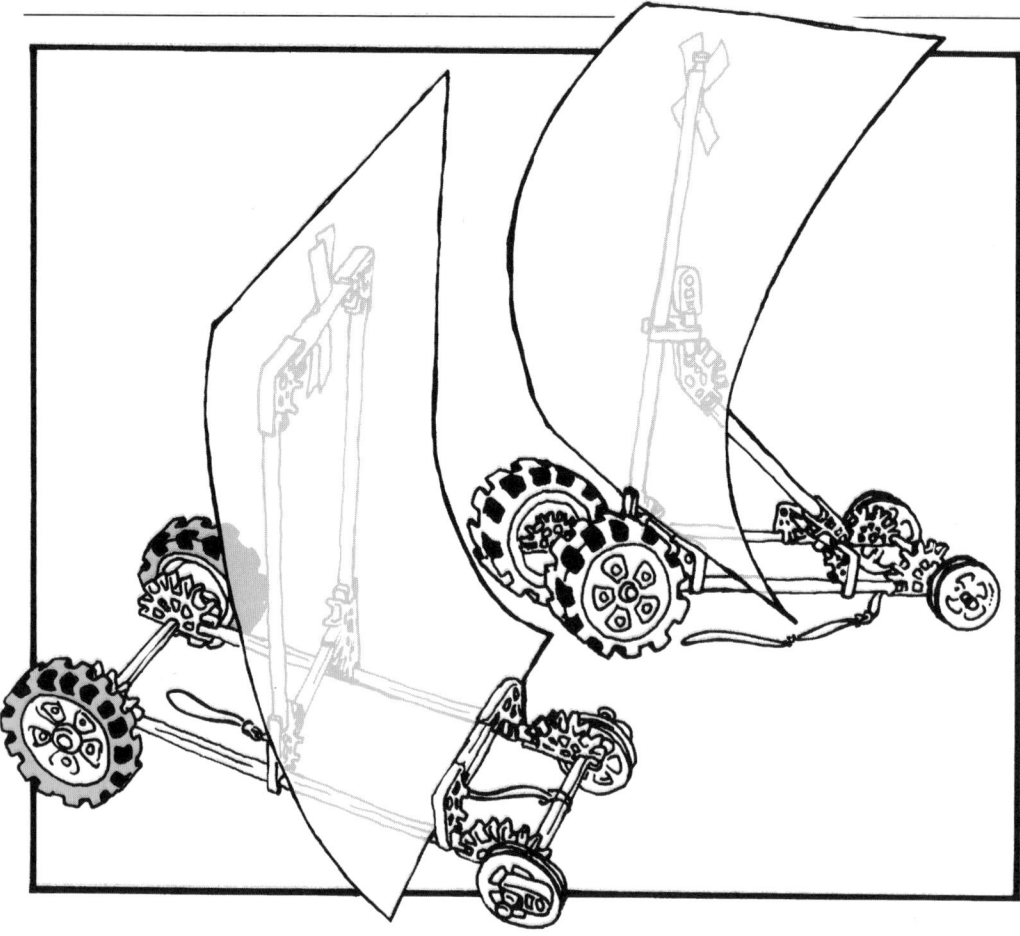

4. Prepare students for **Student Self-Assessment A** by asking them to think about and share with the class what they have learned thus far in the unit.

5. Distribute one copy of the self-assessment to each student. Review each question, but do not elaborate on possible answers. Remind students that this is not a test. It is a way to help them reflect on what they have learned.

6. Have students complete Student Self-Assessment A independently. When they are finished, collect the assessments or have students place them in the pockets of their science notebooks. Let students know they will revisit the self-assessment at the end of the unit. (See Figure 9-2 for student examples.)

Extensions

[LANGUAGE ARTS] [SOCIAL STUDIES] [SCIENCE]

1. Ask students to bring kites of various shapes to school. They can observe how each kite flies on a windy day. Why do the kites fly? Why do some kites fly better than others? Students can also design, build, and test their own kites. Ask students to research the history of the kite. When was it first used? How has it changed over the years?

[SOCIAL STUDIES] [LANGUAGE ARTS]

2. Encourage students to research the history of the sailboat. How has its design changed over the years? How has the use of sails changed? When is a sail a hindrance to the boat's forward motion?

Figure 9-2

Sample Student
Self-Assessment A

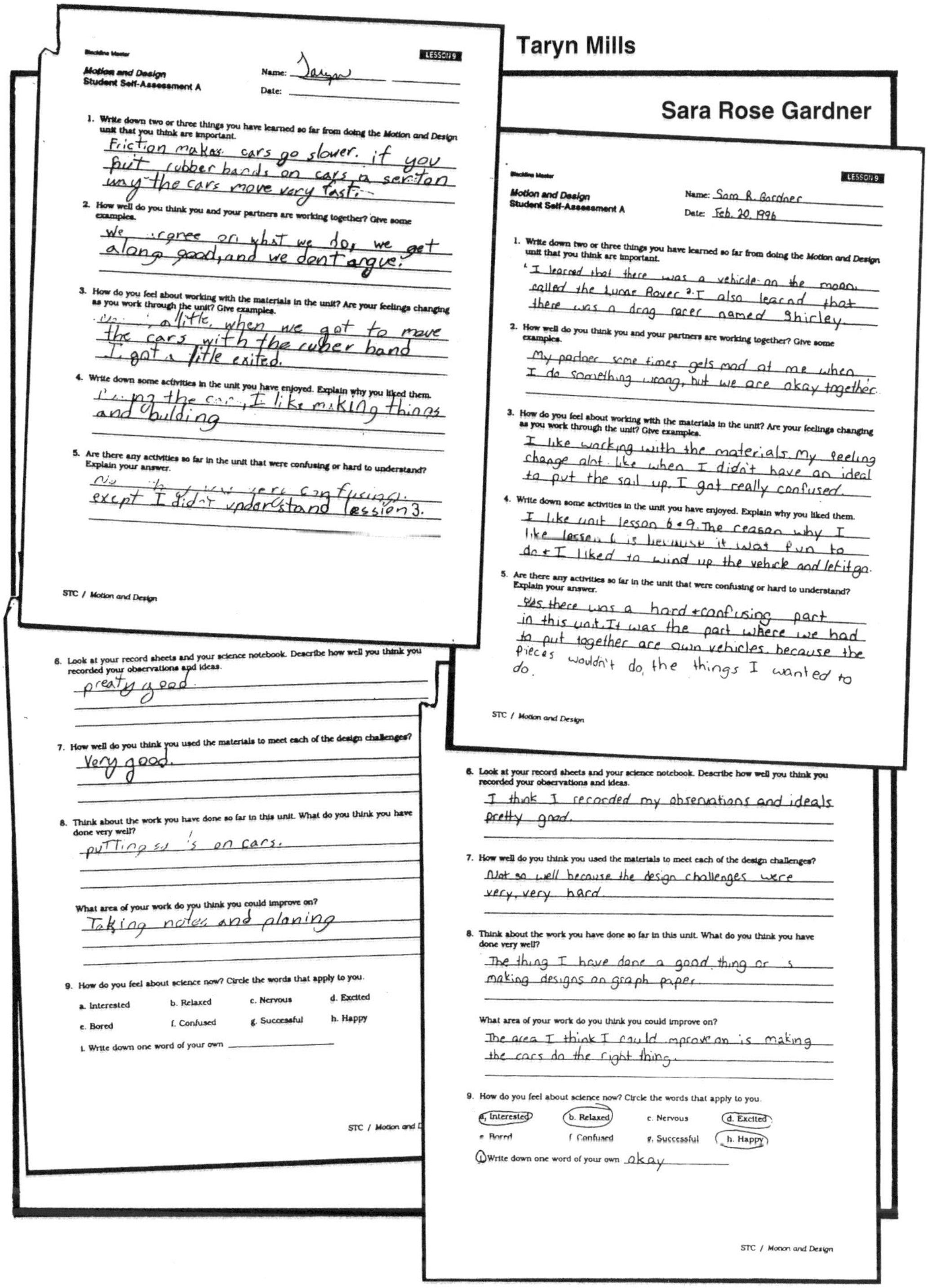

SCIENCE **MATHEMATICS**

3. Students can use an electric fan or a mounted blow dryer to simulate moving a sail-driven vehicle with wind energy. Have them mark the distances their vehicles travel at various wind speeds (different speeds on the fan or blow dryer) and then measure the distances and graph the results.

LESSON 9

Assessment

In this lesson, students completed **Student Self-Assessment A.** You will administer a matching self-assessment at the close of the unit. Compare students' responses on the two assessments to determine areas of growth.

> **Preparation for Lesson 10**
>
> - Students will use their vehicles with a sail in Lesson 10. Make certain they do not disassemble or modify the vehicles between lessons.
>
> - The investigation in Lesson 10 requires a large floor space. If you have access to a resource room, gym, or cafeteria, reserve it ahead of time.

Blackline Master

Motion and Design
Student Self-Assessment A

Name: _____

Date: _____

1. Write down two or three things you have learned so far in the *Motion and Design* unit that you think are important.

   _____
   _____
   _____

2. How well do you think you and your partners are working together? Give some examples.

   _____
   _____
   _____

3. How do you feel about working with the materials in the unit? Are your feelings changing as you work through the unit? Give examples.

   _____
   _____
   _____

4. Write down some activities in the unit you have enjoyed. Explain why you liked them.

   _____
   _____
   _____

5. Are there any activities so far in the unit that are confusing or hard to understand? Explain your answer.

   _____
   _____
   _____

Motion and Design
Student Self-Assessment A, *continued*

Name: _____

6. Look at your record sheets and your science notebook. Describe how well you think you recorded your observations and ideas.

   _____
   _____
   _____

7. How well do you think you used the materials to meet each of the design challenges?

   _____
   _____
   _____

8. Think about the work you have done so far in this unit. What do you think you have done very well?

   _____
   _____
   _____

   In what area of your work do you think you could improve?

   _____
   _____
   _____

9. How do you feel about science now? Circle the words that apply to you.

   a. Interested   b. Relaxed   c. Nervous   d. Excited

   e. Bored   f. Confused   g. Successful   h. Happy

   i. Write down one word of your own _____

LESSON 10

Testing the Effects of Air Resistance on a Vehicle's Motion

Overview and Objectives

In this lesson, students conduct a formal investigation in which they test the effects of air resistance on the motion of their axle-driven vehicles. Using the vehicles they built in Lesson 9, students record the distances the vehicles travel with their cardboard sails catching the air. They make hypotheses about the effect of the sail on the motion of their vehicles and test ways in which they can minimize the influence of the sail on the vehicles' motion. By discussing why the number of turns on the rubber band and the weight of the vehicle should remain constant, students are introduced to the importance of controlling variables. As they discuss the effects of air on the vehicle's motion, students prepare for Lesson 11, in which they build vehicles driven by a rubber band and a propeller.

- Students test how air resistance influences a vehicle's motion.
- Students discuss and compare results.
- Students relate their observations to real-world objects designed to minimize air resistance.
- Through a reading selection, students learn more about racing vehicles that are designed to minimize air resistance and about a woman who was a pioneer in drag racing.

Background

Hold your hand near an open window of a moving car and you can feel the force of the wind pushing it back. This same force pushes on the entire car. However, because the car has a much larger surface area than your hand, the force on the car is much greater.

The force that air exerts on your hand—or on any moving object—is a kind of friction called **air resistance.** Air resistance opposes a vehicle's motion and slows it down. If you hold your hand near the window and the car is moving fast, the force on your hand is much greater than if the car is moving slowly. The force of air resistance increases quite rapidly as the speed of the vehicle increases.

Just as students learned in Lesson 8 that the force of friction between vehicle parts slows the vehicle's motion, they learn in this lesson that the force of friction between the sail and the air opposes the vehicle's motion.

Knowledge of air resistance is critical to engineers who design, build, and test vehicles. They refer to air resistance as **drag.** Designs that minimize drag are known as **aerodynamic.** For example, many automobile shapes are smooth and curved, without sharp corners, much like the nose of an airplane. Designers

LESSON 10

make the front of many cars quite low. From the side, these cars look like a wedge that pushes air up and out of the way as they move. These aerodynamic design features have many practical advantages. They allow vehicles to move faster and save fuel. They are also visually appealing.

Aerodynamic design is important for trucks, too. Figure 10-1 shows a photograph of a moving van. Notice the curved shape on top of the cab. This shape helps the air flow smoothly over the cab and trailer. Without it, the air would hit the flat, vertical wall of the trailer and slow the truck down. The curved surface keeps the air flowing smoothly up and over the truck, reducing air resistance at highway speeds.

Figure 10-1

Airflow over a moving van

The faster a vehicle moves, the more effect air resistance will have on slowing it. Therefore, it is important that students' vehicles in this lesson move fast enough for the force of air resistance to be significant. For this reason, suggest to students that they wind the rubber band 10 or more times around the axle. For results to be comparable, students must use the same number of turns for all trials.

Adding a cardboard sail to the axle-driven vehicles in this lesson changes the surface area and weight of the vehicles. To accurately compare the distances a vehicle travels with and without the sail catching the air, the variable of vehicle weight must be controlled, which means that the sail should not be removed from the vehicles. However, most students at this level are not developmentally ready to fully understand the concept of controlled variables. During the investigation, encourage students to try their own methods for reducing the sail's influence. Some groups might remove the sail from their vehicle, while others will leave the sail on the vehicle, perhaps furling it or turning it sideways, as shown in Figure 10-2. (The latter method ensures that the weight of the vehicle remains the same during all trials.)

Materials

For each student
- 1 science notebook
  Safety goggles

For each group of three students
- 1 vehicle with cardboard sail (from Lesson 9)
- 1 strip of adding machine tape, 4 m (13 ft)
- 3 self-stick red dots, 2 cm (¾ in)
- 3 self-stick blue dots, 2 cm (¾ in)
- 1 bucket of building pieces (with inventory sheet, Building Pieces for Each Group)
- 3 No. 16 rubber bands, connected

Figure 10-2

Sample student vehicles with sail not catching the air

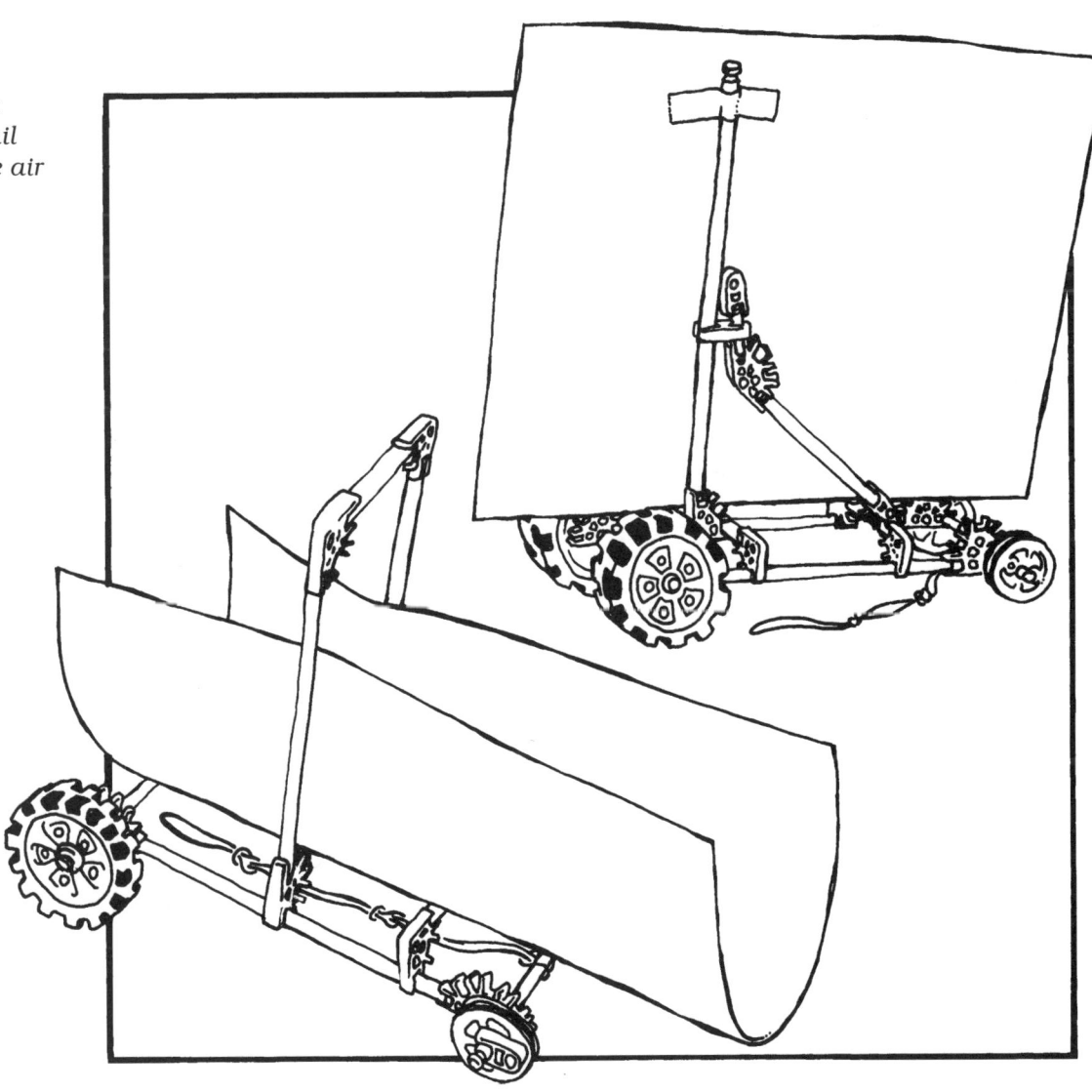

For the class
  Masking tape
  Scissors
  Extra rubber bands, No. 16

Preparation

1. Check the connected rubber bands. If they have become less elastic, replace them with new ones.

2. Cut the adding machine tape into strips that measure 4 m (13 ft). Each group needs one strip.

3. Prepare a large floor area in your classroom where students can test and measure the distances their vehicles travel.

4. Arrange the materials at the distribution center. Set out the rolls of masking tape for students to use when taping down their paper strips. Or cut two 30-cm (12-in) strips for each group and hang them along an edge of the distribution table. Label the tape "Take two strips."

LESSON 10

Procedure

1. Ask students to hypothesize how the upright sail might affect their vehicles' motion. Let them know they will test their hypotheses in this lesson.

2. Review with students the **Student Instructions for Testing Air Resistance** (pgs. 112–13 in this guide and pgs. 44–45 in the Student Activity Book). Discuss the following points:

   - Suggest that students wind their rubber bands 10 or more times, since the results will be more obvious if their vehicles reach a high speed quickly.

   - Ask students why it would be important to wind their rubber bands around the axle the same number of times for each trial.

   - Point out that in Step 12 of the instructions, students will be asked to change the sail so that it has less influence on the vehicle's motion (as shown in Figure 10-2). Make certain at this point that all groups understand what this means (see **Background**). Remind groups that there are many solutions to this problem.

3. Ask students to collect their vehicles and other materials from the distribution center and to conduct the investigation.

Final Activities

1. Invite groups to display their strips of paper. Ask them to discuss what they observed when their vehicles moved with the sail influencing the motion (red dots) and with the sail having less influence on the vehicles' motion (blue dots). What patterns did they notice? What differences? Why do they think this happened?

2. Discuss the ways in which students adapted the sail to have less influence on their vehicles' motion. If any groups kept the sail on their vehicles during the second set of trials—for example, by furling it or turning it sideways—discuss why they chose to do so. Ask students to recall Lesson 4. Why was the weight of the wooden blocks an important factor? Why is the weight of the sail in this lesson an important factor? Why might it be difficult for groups to compare their results in this lesson?

3. Encourage students to relate today's results to the ideas about friction discussed in Lesson 8. For example, how does the sail rubbing or pushing against the air affect the vehicle's motion? Ask students to discuss objects in their lives that have been designed to reduce air resistance. Help students understand that everyday objects, such as cars, boats, bike helmets, and even running clothes, are designed to minimize air resistance.

4. Ask students to clean up. Have them completely disassemble their vehicles and return all building pieces to their buckets. They can return their cardboard sails to the distribution center. Decide if you want students to inventory their building pieces at this time, using the blackline master **Building Pieces for Each Group,** which is stored in their buckets.

Management Tips

- A parent or student volunteer can inventory the building pieces. Make certain the inventory is completed before Lesson 11, when students will need a specific number of pieces of each color to build their vehicles.

- The following step can be completed now or at another time, such as during Language Arts.

5. Assign the reading selection "Shirley Muldowney—Drag Racer" (pgs. 114–15 in this guide and pgs. 46–47 in the Student Activity Book). Ask students to think about how the shape of Shirley Muldowney's vehicle affected its motion. Students should record their ideas in their notebooks.

Extensions

MATHEMATICS

1. Have students use the 100-cm (39-in) tape to measure the distances of all the dots in this investigation. Ask students to select the measurement (dot on the paper strip) that best represents the three distances their vehicles traveled for each part of the investigation. This measurement might be the distance of the middle dot, the distance where the dots clustered, or the greatest distance. Students can record the measurements in a table similar to the one below.

Figure 10-3

Sample data table

Sail's Influence	Distance Traveled (in cm)			Selected Distance
	Trial 1	Trial 2	Trial 3	
Sail influencing vehicle's motion				
Sail having less influence on vehicle's motion				

MATHEMATICS

2. Challenge students to graph their data from Extension 1.

LANGUAGE ARTS

3. Ask students to imagine they are pirates seeking sunken treasure in the middle of the Great Blue Sea. Their pirate vessel is the only hope of getting to the treasure. But a violent storm with gusting winds has come up and their vessel is moving in the wrong direction. What will they do? Write a story telling the tale.

SCIENCE

4. Challenge students to use materials other than cardboard to make sails. How does the material affect the vehicle's design? Ask students to hypothesize how each material will affect their vehicles' motion. Then have them test their hypotheses.

Preparation for Lesson 11

- Solicit the help of an adult volunteer to build the propeller units for Lesson 11. See Lesson 11, **Preparation** Step 1 for directions. For safety reasons, wear goggles. This task should not be completed by students.

- Make certain students have disassembled the vehicles they used in this lesson.

LESSON 10

Student Instructions for Testing Air Resistance

1. Find an area on the floor where your vehicle can move a long distance.
2. Roll out your strip of paper. Tape it to the floor. Use masking tape to make a starting line at one end of the paper strip.
3. Make certain that the cardboard sail is tightly attached to your vehicle.
4. Discuss with your group how you think the sail will influence your vehicle's motion. Record your group's ideas in your notebook. Remember to date your entry.

5. Decide how many times you will wind the rubber band around the axle, but it must be *at least 10 times.* (Be careful! The rubber band will break if you wind it too many times.) Record the number you choose in your notebook. Use this number every time you wind the rubber band in this lesson.
6. Wear your safety goggles. Using the number you decided on, wind the rubber band around the free-spinning axle of your vehicle. Put your vehicle's small front wheels on the starting line.
7. Let go of the vehicle. Observe its motion.
8. Put a **red** dot on the paper strip where the front wheels of the vehicle stopped.

9. Repeat this test two more times.
   - Wind the rubber band around the axle the same number of times for each trial.
   - Let go of the car.
   - How far did your vehicle move? Mark the stopping point with a red dot.

112 / Testing the Effects of Air Resistance on a Vehicle's Motion   STC / *Motion and Design*

10. When you have tested your vehicle three times, look at the three red dots. Are the distances your vehicle traveled close together? Are they spread out? Why do you think this happened? Record your observations in your notebook.

11. Which dot do you think best represents all the distances your vehicle traveled? Circle that dot with a pencil.

12. Discuss with your group how you could change the sail so it has less influence on the vehicle's motion. Write your ideas in your notebook. Then change the sail with your group.

13. With your group, predict how the change made to the sail will affect the vehicle's motion. Record your group's prediction in your notebook.

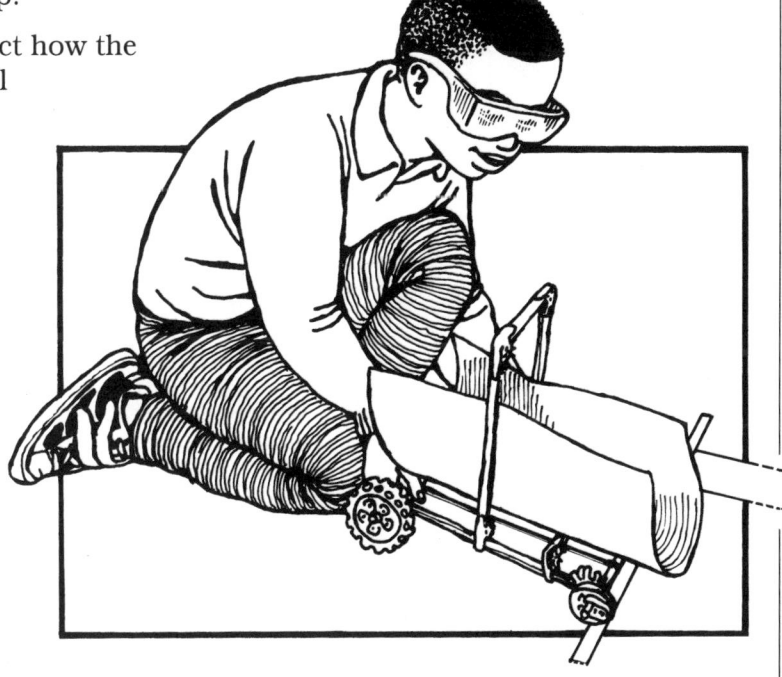

14. Test how far your modified vehicle will travel, but this time, use the **blue** dots. Remember to do the following:

    ■ Put the vehicle's front wheels on the starting line.

    ■ Wind the rubber band the same number of times as earlier in the investigation.

    ■ Let go of the vehicle.

    ■ Mark the distance your vehicle traveled. Put a blue dot on the paper strip where the front wheels of the vehicle stopped. Do this three times altogether. When you finish, there should be three blue dots and three red dots on the paper strip.

15. Discuss the results with your group. How did the sail influence the motion of your axle-driven vehicle? Why do you think this happened? Record your observations in your notebook.

Reading Selection

Shirley Muldowney—Drag Racer

Have you ever been to a drag race? Just imagine—the roar of engines, the whoosh of air as cars speed by, the screams and cheers of the crowd. Shirley Muldowney knows all about drag racing. In fact, she races dragsters. What exactly is a dragster? It's a lightweight, powerful vehicle with up to four engines mounted on a long, narrow frame. To reduce air resistance, the dragster has a smooth, aerodynamic body. In a drag race, two cars at a time race on a straight, quarter-mile track. The cars go very fast—often 250 miles per hour! And they make a lot of noise. The first car at the finish line wins.

Shirley Muldowney began racing in the 1970s. Many people felt she would never succeed. "A woman racer?" they said. "No way!" But Shirley proved them wrong.

Faster and faster she went until, in 1977 and 1980, she won the National Hot Rod Association championship. She became famous and was featured in magazine articles and television commercials. Her life story was even made into a movie called *Heart Like a Wheel*.

Then disaster struck. While racing in Canada, Shirley Muldowney had a terrible accident. The inner tube from one of her car's front tires blew out, and her car broke into pieces. Shirley was badly hurt. Some people thought she would never walk again. Everyone assumed Shirley's racing career was over. It took her many months to recover. But Shirley was determined to come back.

With hard work and practice, Shirley raced again. She even continued to finish among the top 10 drivers in the country. When asked why she returned to drag racing, Shirley replied, "It's what I do."

Shirley Muldowney showed what skill and determination can accomplish. She wanted to race and decided to let nothing stand in her way. Other women have benefited from her experience. Thanks to Shirley, more and more women compete in drag racing all the time.

LESSON 11   Building a Propeller-Driven Vehicle

Overview and Objectives

In Lesson 6, students were introduced to the concept that energy can be stored in a twisted rubber band. In Lesson 10, they observed the effects of air resistance on the motion of an axle-driven vehicle. This lesson extends students' understanding of these two concepts by asking them to build a vehicle with a propeller. Students use a technical drawing to build propeller-driven vehicles and then make initial observations about their design features. They also compare their vehicles with the axle-driven vehicles they built in earlier lessons. These experiences prepare students for Lesson 12, in which they analyze specific design features of their vehicles and discuss the influence of stored energy and air on the motion of their vehicles.

- Students brainstorm what they know about propeller-driven vehicles.
- Students discuss design features they think are needed for propeller-driven vehicles.
- Students build propeller-driven vehicles from a technical drawing.
- Students discuss their initial observations.

Background

Propellers create a force that moves airplanes and boats forward. Even when an airplane is on the ground, the force from the spinning propellers enables it to taxi on and off the runway. Airboats are propeller-driven vehicles that skim over shallow water. Because the propeller blades are in the air, not the water, these vehicles can move over water less than 30 cm (1 ft) deep.

When a propeller mounted on a vehicle spins, its blades push the air backward, like a fan. In an equal and opposite reaction, as described by Newton's third law, the air pushed backward causes the propeller and its attachments to move forward. A close look at the propeller used in this lesson shows how the blades curve. The force of air against the spinning, curved blades pushes the vehicle forward (see Figure 11-1).

In this lesson, students use a technical drawing to build a vehicle that has a twisted rubber band attached to a propeller. As students turn the propeller, they store energy in the rubber band. Students will notice a regular series of knots of identical size forming in the rubber band as they tighten it, as shown in Figure 11-2. Letting go of the propeller releases the stored energy, spins the propeller blades, pushes air back, and pushes the vehicle forward.

Each time students wind their propellers another turn, the amount of energy stored in the rubber band increases. When they release the propeller, the stored energy changes to energy of motion of the vehicle and the turbulent air. Initially,

LESSON 11

Figure 11-1

Looking at a propeller

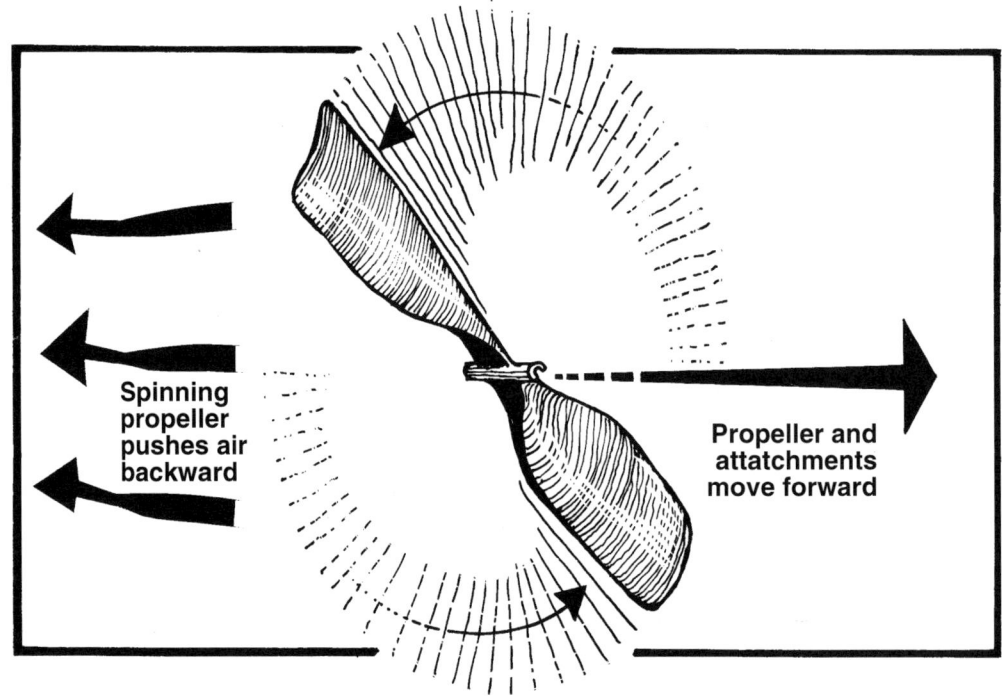

Figure 11-2

Storing energy in a rubber band

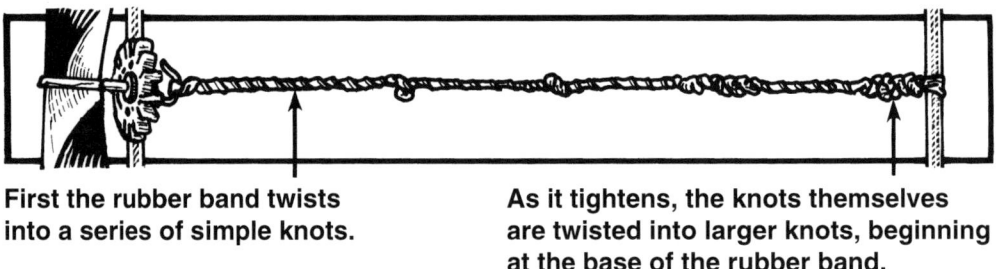

the vehicle might move with a burst of speed. This is because the rubber band is at its maximum tension. When first released, the rubber band produces the greatest force and therefore the highest propeller speed.

Propellers must be strong enough to withstand high speeds and great force. Airplane designers must carefully match the size, shape, and number of blades with the aircraft and its engine to ensure top performance and safety. As each group observes its propeller-driven vehicle in this lesson, encourage them to look at how they mounted the propeller on the vehicle and to discuss why it is positioned in this way. For example, students may notice that the propeller is mounted high so the blades can turn freely without hitting the table below. Initial observations like these will help students prepare for Lesson 12, in which they evaluate specific design features of the propeller-driven vehicle and compare the vehicle's design with that of the axle-driven vehicle.

LESSON 11

Materials

For each student
- 1 science notebook
- Safety goggles

For each group of three students
- 1 propeller unit (includes propeller, screw hook, brass eyelets, and white connector)
- 1 bucket of building pieces
- 3 No. 64 rubber bands, connected

For the class
- Materials for teacher to assemble propeller units:
  - 10 propellers
  - 10 hooks
  - 20 brass eyelets
  - 10 white connectors (from students' buckets or class bucket)
- Bucket of extra building pieces
- 1 sheet of newsprint
- Assorted colored markers
- Masking tape
- Trade books, photographs, or illustrations showing propeller-driven vehicles

Preparation

1. If you have not already done so, assemble one propeller unit for each group. Use Figure 11-3 as a guide. For each propeller unit you will need one propeller, two brass eyelets, one white connector, and one hook. Students will attach the three connected rubber bands to the propeller unit's hook after they build their vehicles. Note that the flared ends of the two brass eyelets are on the same side of the white connector. These ends rub together as the propeller spins. Make sure that the hook faces the concave (dished in) side of the propeller blades. The hub (center of the propeller) is rounded on one end and has a tiny corkscrew on the other. The hook goes into the rounded end. Turn the hook clockwise about six turns in the propeller hub. When the hook becomes very difficult to turn, it is seated. The plastic around the hook will lighten in color. Check to be sure the plastic shaft, or opening on the propeller into which the hook attaches, has not split.

2. Using the class bucket of building pieces and the technical drawing from Lesson 2 (pg. 36), build a standard vehicle that you will use in the **Final Activities.** Attach a connected rubber band to the axle.

3. To familiarize yourself with the building process students will engage in during this lesson, assemble a propeller-driven vehicle using the technical drawing in Figure 11-4.

4. Label the sheet of newsprint "Design Ideas for Propeller-Driven Vehicles." Date and hang the sheet.

5. Collect and display trade books, photographs, or illustrations that show propeller-driven vehicles.

6. Connect three large rubber bands. Each group needs one set of connected rubber bands.

7. Arrange the rubber bands, safety goggles, buckets of building pieces, and propeller units at the distribution center. Using an index card, label the propeller units "Take one."

LESSON 11

Figure 11-3

Preparing the propellers

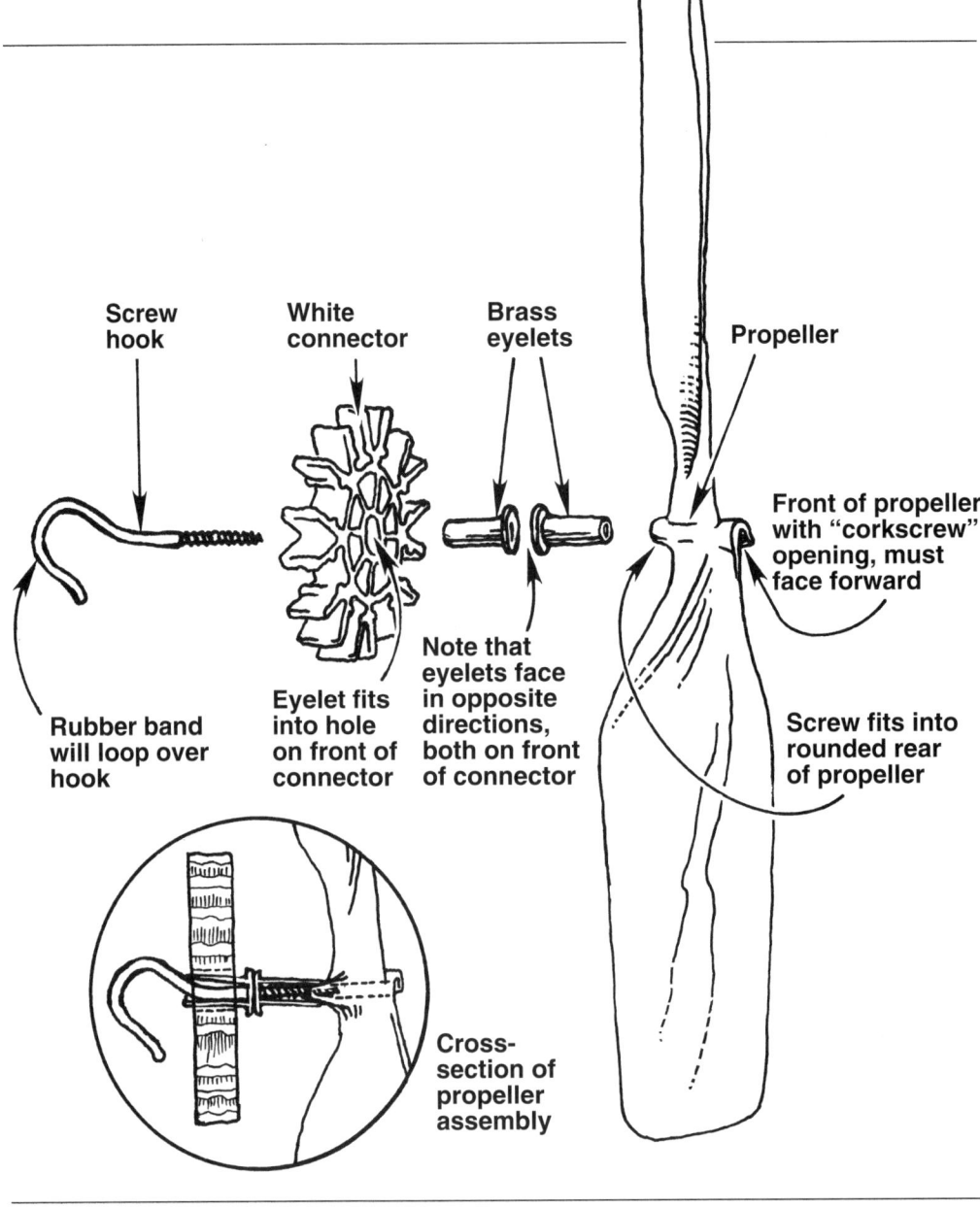

Procedure

1. Involve students in a brainstorming session in which they describe what they know about propeller-driven vehicles. Let students know that they will use a technical drawing to build a propeller-driven vehicle in this lesson. They will analyze its design features in Lesson 12.

2. Focus students' attention on one of the assembled propeller units. Point out the white connector and how the connected rubber bands attach to the propeller hook. Ask students to think about how the white connector could be used to attach the propeller to the vehicle and where on the vehicle the rubber band could be connected.

3. Ask students to think about vehicle design features that might be necessary to move their vehicles with a propeller. Encourage them to share their ideas. For example, students might say the propeller must be high in the air so it will not hit the ground as it spins. Others might suggest that the propeller must be in the front or that the rubber band must be taut and connected straight across from the propeller. List their design ideas on the sheet of newsprint titled "Design Ideas for Propeller-Driven Vehicles."

Figure 11-4

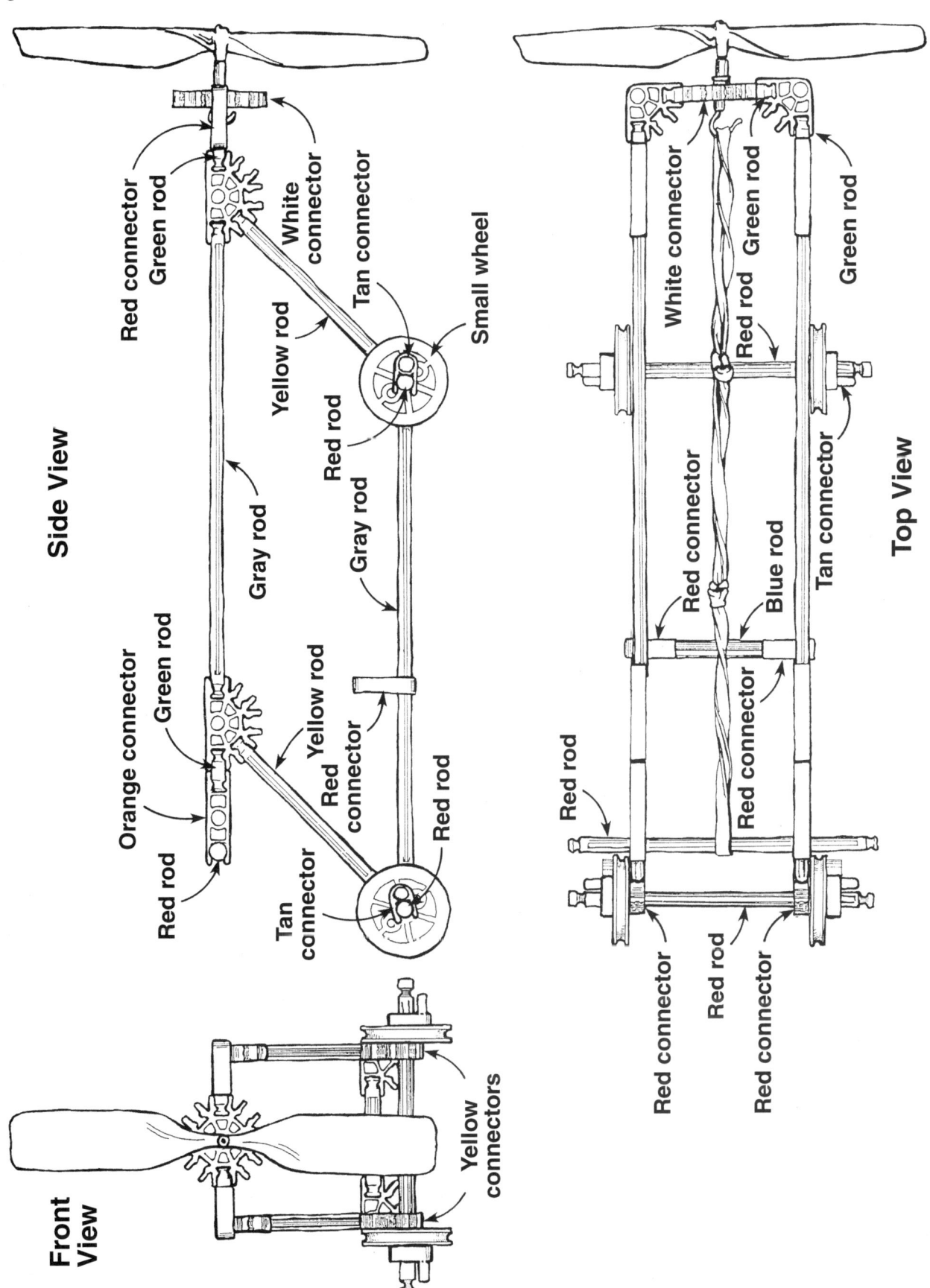

Building a Propeller-Driven Vehicle

LESSON 11

4. Direct students' attention to the technical drawing of the propeller-driven vehicle (Figure 11-4 on pg. 121 in this guide and Figure 11-1 on pg. 48 in the Student Activity Book). Ask students to describe how this drawing is different from the one used in Lesson 2. If students do not mention it, point out that the drawing is a three-view technical drawing that not only shows the vehicle from the side and top (as in Lesson 2) but also from the front. Ask students why a front view might be necessary for building a propeller-driven vehicle.

5. Have each group collect its bucket of building pieces, propeller unit, safety goggles, and connected rubber bands from the distribution center and begin building the propeller-driven vehicle using Figure 11-4 as their guide.

> **Safety Note:** Students *must* wear safety goggles in this lesson. The goggles will prevent injury in the event the rubber band slips off the hook or the hook comes out of the propeller. Teachers and adult volunteers should also wear safety goggles when working with the propeller units or the propeller-driven vehicles.

6. After students finish building, encourage them to try to move the propeller-driven vehicles. Ask groups to record in their notebooks any general observations they have about their vehicle's motion.

Final Activities

1. Invite students to present their completed vehicles to the class. Have them discuss any difficulties or successes they had while building from the three-view technical drawing. In what ways was it easier to build from the drawing in this lesson than it was in Lesson 2? In what ways was it more difficult?

2. Have students share their observations about the motion and design of their propeller-driven vehicles by asking questions such as the following:

   - How did you get the vehicle to move?
   - How did you get the propeller to spin?
   - What happened to the rubber band as you wound the propeller?
   - What happened when you let go of the propeller? Why do you think this happened?

3. Show the students the axle-driven vehicle that you built for this lesson. Have students compare their propeller-driven vehicles from this lesson with the axle-driven vehicle by asking the following questions:

   - How is the use of the rubber band with the propeller-driven vehicle and the axle-driven vehicle the same? (energy to move the vehicle stored in rubber band, vehicle moves when energy is released)
   - How is the rubber band used differently? (rubber band is twisted on propeller-driven vehicle, not wrapped around an axle; rubber band moves the propeller, not the axle)

4. Ask students to look at the class brainstorming list "Design Ideas for Propeller-Driven Vehicles." Have students add to or change statements on the list on the basis of their observations in this lesson. Let students know they will analyze the design features of their vehicles in greater detail in Lesson 12.

LESSON 11

5. Have students label their vehicles. Ask them to return their vehicles and other materials to the distribution center. Do not disassemble the axle-driven vehicle you built during the **Preparation.** You can use it again in Lesson 12 for comparison with the propeller-driven vehicle.

Extensions

MATHEMATICS

1. Have students use self-stick dots and a 4-m (13-ft) strip of adding machine tape to test how far their vehicles will move with various turns on the propeller (for example 30, 50, and 75 turns). Have students use a 100-cm (39-in) tape to measure the three distances. Students can measure the distances from the starting line to each dot and record the distance (in cm) on a data table similar to the one in Figure 11-5. They can then select and record the average distance traveled.

Figure 11-5

Sample data table

Number of Turns of the Propeller	Distance Traveled (in cm)			Selected Distance
	Trial 1	Trial 2	Trial 3	
35				
50				
75				

MATHEMATICS

2. Have students graph the selected distances from Extension 1.

SCIENCE

3. Arrange a field trip to a general aviation airport or to a museum that displays propeller airplanes. Encourage students to compare the airplanes they see with the vehicles they built in this lesson.

MATHEMATICS

4. Challenge students to use a timer to measure how long it takes the propeller to spin down after winding it various numbers of turns. Students can graph their results.

Preparation for Lesson 12

Students need their propeller-driven vehicles for Lesson 12. Do not disassemble the axle-driven vehicle you built during the **Preparation** in this lesson. You will use it again during the **Final Activities** of Lesson 12.

STC / *Motion and Design* Building a Propeller-Driven Vehicle / **123**

LESSON 12	**Analyzing the Motion and Design of a Propeller-Driven Vehicle**

Overview and Objectives

In Lesson 11, students built propeller-driven vehicles and made initial observations about their design and motion. In this lesson, students analyze the design features of their propeller-driven vehicles, including frame size and rigidity, and how the features affect propeller movement. Students also revisit the discussion from Lesson 11 in which they compared the motion and design of their propeller-driven vehicles with vehicles tested earlier in the unit. This lesson prepares students for Lesson 13, in which they analyze the cost of their propeller-driven vehicles and redesign them to reduce cost without affecting performance.

- Students analyze the features of propeller-driven vehicles.

- Students discuss the motion and design of their propeller-driven vehicles and compare these features with those of vehicles built previously.

- Students propose design changes for their propeller-driven vehicles that will not affect performance.

Background

Several factors affect how far and fast students' propeller-driven vehicles move in this lesson. Students may note that the rate at which they turn the propeller has no effect on the distance their vehicles travel. However, the more times they wind the propeller and its attached rubber band, the farther the vehicle will move. Moreover, the propeller will spin longer and move the vehicle farther if the rubber band is stretched tightly. Reducing the tension by adding a fourth rubber band to the end of the three connected ones, by contrast, will cause the vehicle to move less efficiently.

In this lesson, students add tires to their propeller-driven vehicles. In Lesson 8, tires enabled students' vehicles to move forward, whereas in this lesson, tires prevent the vehicles from moving easily. Because the propeller-driven vehicle contains more parts, it weighs more than vehicles built earlier. Added weight, including the weight of tires, makes the vehicle more difficult to move using a two-blade propeller.

Students may find that having a smooth surface over which the propeller-driven vehicles can move makes it easier to get the vehicles moving. Carpet may oppose the vehicles' motion due to increased friction with the wheels, while a vinyl or tile surface will facilitate motion.

In their analysis, students may find that the direction in which they turn the propeller (clockwise or counterclockwise) determines the direction the vehicles move. The placement of the propeller (high or low, front or back) and the angle created by the rubber band when students connect it to their vehicles can also

STC / *Motion and Design*

LESSON 12

affect the vehicle's motion. If a group mounts its propeller high on the vehicle, it can spin freely, without hitting the wheels or the surface over which it moves. However, if building pieces protrude from the vehicle's frame, the propeller may hit these pieces and will not spin freely. If the rubber band is mounted at an angle on the vehicle, the propeller will be at an angle as well. An angled propeller will move air downward, instead of straight back, resulting in a less-efficient propulsion system.

At the close of the lesson, students are asked to compare the motion and design of their propeller-driven vehicles with axle-driven vehicles they built earlier. They may note some of the following similarities and differences.

- The propeller-driven vehicles store energy in the same way as axle-driven vehicles—in a rubber band.

- Students mount the rubber band on the propeller-driven vehicle in a new way.

- Students store energy in the rubber band on the propeller-driven vehicle by turning the propeller. For axle-driven vehicles, they stored energy in the rubber band by winding it around an axle.

- When students release the rubber band on the propeller-driven vehicle, it spins a propeller. When they released it on axle-driven vehicles, it turned the axle and the wheels attached to it.

- On a propeller-driven vehicle, air pushing backward from the spinning propeller moves the vehicle forward. On the axle-driven vehicle with a sail, air pushing against the sail slowed the vehicle's forward motion.

Assessing the effects of design features such as these on the motion of propeller-driven vehicles and applying knowledge from previous lessons is the primary focus of this lesson.

Materials

For each student
- 1 science notebook
- 1 pencil with eraser
- Safety goggles

For each group of three students
- 1 copy of **Record Sheet 12-A: What Happens If . . .**
- 1 propeller-driven vehicle, with connected rubber bands attached (from Lesson 11)
- 1 bucket of building pieces

For the class
- 9 No. 64 rubber bands
- Brainstorming list, "Design Ideas for Propeller-Driven Vehicles" (from Lesson 11)
- Assorted colored markers
- Masking tape

LESSON 12

Preparation

1. Make one copy of **Record Sheet 12-A: What Happens If . . .** for each group (or student).

2. Using six rubber bands, create two extra sets of connected No. 64 rubber bands. Put the two sets of connected No. 64 rubber bands aside for groups that decide to complete the last question on the record sheet. Or place the two extra sets of rubber bands on the distribution center and label them "Take as needed." Also set out three *individual* No. 64 rubber bands for groups that complete the next to the last question on the record sheet.

3. Arrange the vehicles, connected rubber bands, individual rubber bands, safety goggles, and buckets of building pieces on the distribution center. Label each.

4. Display the brainstorming list from Lesson 11. Set out markers of a different color from the writing on the list.

5. Preview the record sheet and try several "What if . . ." questions on your own before beginning the lesson. Because students are asked to complete only three or more questions on the record sheet, you may want to set up a center with a propeller-driven vehicle and the class bucket of building pieces. Students can complete unfinished "What if . . ." questions during center time. They can also create their own "What if . . ." questions for other students to analyze at the center.

Procedure

1. Let students know they will analyze several design features of their propeller-driven vehicles in this lesson.

2. Distribute **Record Sheet 12-A: What Happens If . . .** to each group (or student). Discuss how students are to use the record sheet to evaluate the design features of their propeller-driven vehicles. Remind students of the following:

   - Complete the "What if . . ." questions in any order you choose.

   - Remove pieces and modify your vehicle as needed for each "What if . . ." question, but return your vehicle to its original form after each test.

   - Although you are only asked to complete three questions, do as many as you can in the time given.

   - Try to come up with your own "What if . . ." question and test it.

3. Have each group collect its vehicle and bucket of building pieces from the distribution center. An extra set of connected rubber bands and an individual rubber band are needed only for the last two "What if . . ." questions. Students should collect these items only if they test those particular questions. Remind them to return the rubber bands to the distribution center when they are finished, so that other groups may use them.

4. Allow students time to complete the investigation.

Final Activities

1. Ask students to discuss the observations they recorded on the record sheet. Students may want to demonstrate some of their results, since groups may have tested different questions.

Management Tip: If you have a large class, you may want to combine two or three groups into one team and have groups share results with the team, instead of the entire class.

STC / *Motion and Design*   Analyzing the Motion and Design of a Propeller-Driven Vehicle / **127**

LESSON 12

2. Show students the axle-driven vehicle. Ask students to revisit the discussion from Lesson 11 in which they compared the design and motion of the propeller-driven vehicles with vehicles built in previous lessons. Use questions such as the following:

   - What caused the propeller-driven vehicle to move?
   - What happened to the rubber band as you wound the propeller?
   - Think back to previous lessons. What caused the axle-driven vehicle to move?
   - In what ways is the rubber band used differently in this lesson? In what ways is it used in the same way?
   - How is air involved in moving the propeller-driven vehicle?

3. Focus students' attention on the brainstorming list from Lesson 11, "Design Ideas for Propeller-Driven Vehicles." What can they add to or change on the list? Which questions on **Record Sheet 12-A: What Happens If . . .** support their ideas?

4. Ask students to clean up. Make certain all vehicles are labeled with the group letter.

Extensions

SOCIAL STUDIES **LANGUAGE ARTS**

1. Have students research how the Wright brothers powered their aircraft.

SCIENCE

2. Ask students to collect toy vehicles that have propellers and analyze the design features of each. How are the propellers on the toy vehicles the same as or different from those used in this lesson?

SOCIAL STUDIES **ART**

3. Ask students to research and report on the flying machines designed by Leonardo da Vinci. Students can create models of these flying machines with paper.

Assessment

In Lessons 11 and 12, students built on the concepts of motion and the skills of design by building and evaluating a propeller-driven vehicle. As you assess student's concepts, skills, and attitudes in these two lessons, keep in mind the following questions.

Concepts and Skills

- In what ways does the student describe the motion of the propeller-driven vehicle?

- In the student's verbal contributions to the group and class, does he or she describe or convey an intuitive understanding that a spinning propeller exerts a force against the air, which may result in the motion of the vehicle?

- Can the student apply an understanding of stored energy to the use of a rubber band to spin the propeller?

- Can the student build, with the group, a vehicle from a three-view drawing, using the skills acquired in Lesson 2 and applied throughout the unit?

LESSON 12

- When evaluating the design of the vehicle in Lesson 12, does the student identify the features of the propeller-driven vehicle that affect its function?

Attitudes

- Does the student recognize and appreciate the role that technological design plays in analyzing the design features of a vehicle? Can the student apply the information discussed to real propeller-driven vehicles?

- When analyzing design features in Lesson 12, does the student develop a respect for test results and for using those results to improve design?

LESSON 12

Record Sheet 12–A   Names: _____

Date: _____

What Happens If . . .

Look at your propeller-driven vehicle. Pick three or more of the following questions to test. Test them in any order you choose. Try to move your vehicle after each change you make. Record your observations in the space provided. Remember to return the vehicle to its standard form after each question.

What happens if . . .

- . . . you wind the propeller 30 times quickly? What happens if you wind it 30 times slowly? How does the vehicle move each time?

  _____
  _____
  _____

- . . . you wind the propeller clockwise 30 times? What happens if you wind it counterclockwise 30 times? How does the vehicle move each time?

  _____
  _____
  _____

- . . . you turn the vehicle around so the propeller is on the back of the vehicle?

  _____
  _____
  _____

- . . . you change the position of the rubber band so it is attached at an angle?

  _____
  _____
  _____

- . . . you add tires to the propeller-driven vehicle?

  _____
  _____
  _____

STC / *Motion and Design*

Record Sheet 12–A   Names: _____

_____

_____

LESSON 12

What Happens If . . ., *continued*

- . . . you move the vehicle on a different surface, such as carpet or vinyl?

  _____
  _____
  _____

- . . . you place the propeller lower on the vehicle? (Modify the vehicle so the propeller is closer to the ground.)

  _____
  _____
  _____

- . . . you use four connected rubber bands instead of three? (Attach another rubber band to the three connected ones and then test the vehicle.)

  _____
  _____
  _____

- . . . you use two parallel sets of rubber bands on the vehicle? (Put two sets of three connected rubber bands, side-by-side, on the vehicle. Now test the vehicle.)

  _____
  _____
  _____

Now write and test one of your own questions.

- What happens if . . .

  _____
  _____
  _____

STC / *Motion and Design*

LESSON 13

Looking at Cost

Overview and Objectives

Thus far in the unit, students have designed, built, evaluated, and modified vehicles to meet specific design requirements. They have used these vehicles to investigate various principles of motion. In this lesson, students learn about a totally different design requirement—cost. By adding the price of each part, students determine the total cost of their propeller-driven vehicles. Then they redesign their vehicles to reduce cost while maintaining performance. Working within a budget prepares students for the final design challenge in Lessons 14 through 16.

- Students determine the cost of their propeller-driven vehicles.
- Students modify their vehicles to reduce cost.
- Students evaluate the strength and performance of their modified vehicles.
- Students discuss trade-offs involving vehicle cost, performance, and appearance.

Background

Cost is an important design requirement for most manufactured products. If a product costs too much, it will not sell. To minimize cost, designers remove unnecessary parts, especially expensive ones, so that the product represents the best value, or the best performance at the lowest cost. Consider, for example, a radio tower that must withstand high winds and occasional storms. Before adding bracing to the design, the engineer evaluates the cost of various types of bracing and builds models to evaluate their effectiveness. For the bracing to be **cost-effective,** the project manager usually chooses to use the most effective bracing available at the lowest cost.

Vehicle manufacturers design their products to sell at competitive prices. Auto designers remove unnecessary parts or material. However, identifying unnecessary automobile parts is much more difficult than identifying needed radio tower parts, because many of the auto parts—air conditioners, for instance—provide comfort or conveniences that customers demand.

By conducting surveys and discussion groups, automobile companies learn as much as possible about the people who buy their cars. How much engine power do customers want? What gasoline mileage do they require? What about extra features to make a car more comfortable? After the company identifies the needs of customers, designers try to balance those needs with all the design characteristics of the car to make a desirable product at a low price.

An automotive engineer has many options for improving design. A more efficient engine will increase gas mileage as well as maintain top speed and acceleration.

LESSON 13

An aerodynamic shape will decrease wind noise and increase gas mileage. If designers can incorporate these improvements at a reasonable cost, a car will be appealing as well as affordable. Engineers repeatedly review each part and system of a newly designed car with the goal of reducing cost without compromising quality. To evaluate a proposed change, they build a model and test whether it meets the requirements. In this lesson, students will take on that same challenge.

Materials

For each student
- 1 science notebook
- 1 pencil with eraser
- Safety goggles

For each group of three students
- 2 copies of **Record Sheet 13-A: Evaluating the Cost of Our Design**
- 1 propeller-driven vehicle (from Lesson 11)
- 1 bucket of building pieces (with inventory sheet)
- 1 calculator (optional)

For the class
- 1 sheet of newsprint
- Assorted colored markers

Preparation

1. Make two copies of **Record Sheet 13-A: Evaluating the Cost of Our Design** for each group.
2. Title the sheet of newsprint "How We Can Reduce the Cost of Our Vehicles."
3. Decide if students will use calculators to compute the cost of their vehicles. If so, acquire them before beginning the lesson.
4. Arrange the materials at the distribution center.
5. Preview the lesson. Decide if you need one session or two to complete it. An appropriate stopping point is suggested between **Procedure** Steps 6 and 7.

Procedure

1. Ask students to recall the various requirements they have met in designing vehicles thus far in the unit. Challenge students to think of other requirements that engineers might need to meet.
2. If students do not mention it, point out that cost is often a requirement when engineers design and build a product. Let students know they will determine the cost of their propeller-driven vehicles, modify the vehicles to reduce cost, test them to make certain they still perform well, and then determine the final cost of the modified vehicles.
3. Distribute two copies of **Record Sheet 13-A: Evaluating the Cost of Our Design** to each group. Using one group's vehicle as an example, discuss how to complete the record sheet.
4. Have each group pick up its vehicle from the distribution center and determine its cost using one of the record sheets as an aide. If you are using calculators, distribute them at this time.

5. After students complete Record Sheet 13-A, ask them to present the cost of their vehicles to the class. Discuss why the cost for all groups is similar or the same. Have students use this number as the vehicle's average cost. Invite students to determine, on the basis of the average cost, what they would consider to be an "inexpensive" vehicle. What would they consider to be an "expensive" vehicle?

6. Ask students to brainstorm possible changes they could make to reduce the cost of their propeller-driven vehicles. List all ideas on the sheet titled "How To Reduce Vehicle Cost." A sample class list is shown in Figure 13-1.

Figure 13-1

How one class reduced vehicle cost

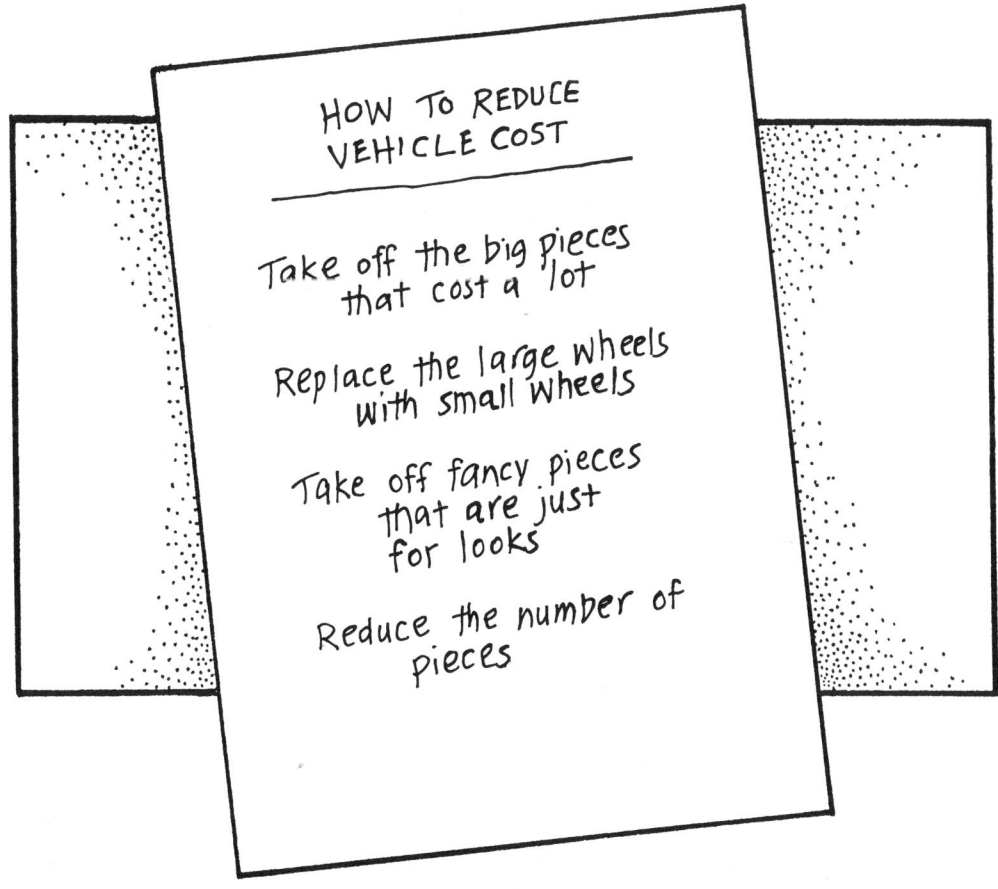

Management Tip: If you need to divide this lesson into two sessions, this is a good stopping point.

7. Invite students to redesign and modify their propeller-driven vehicles to reduce total cost without affecting performance. Students should test the strength and motion of their modified vehicles to make certain they will move using the propeller.

8. Ask students to determine the cost of their modified vehicles. Remind them to use the second copy of the record sheet for this step. An example is shown in Figure 13-2.

LESSON 13

Figure 13-2

Sample cost sheets from one group

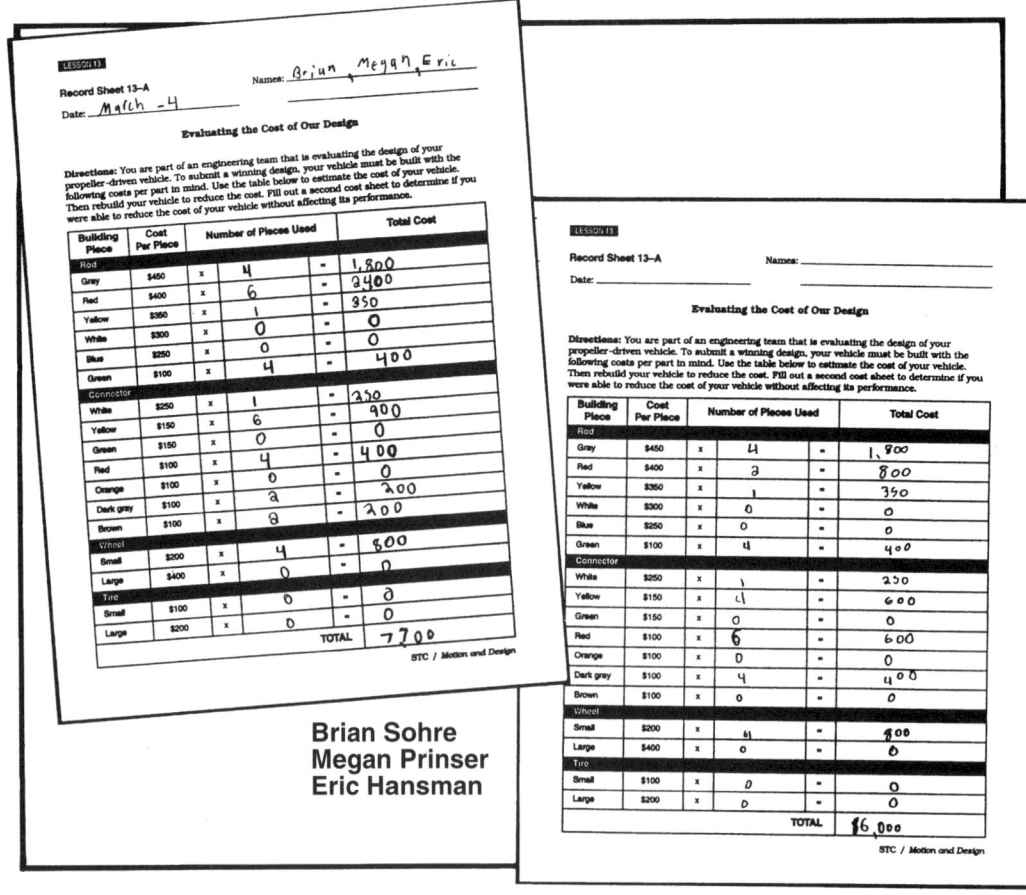

Brian Sohre
Megan Prinser
Eric Hansman

Final Activities

1. Discuss with students the effects of reducing vehicle cost. Ask questions such as the following:
   - How did you reduce the cost of your vehicle?
   - How much money did you save?
   - At any point, did reducing the vehicle's cost affect your vehicle's appearance? Describe what you did in this situation.
   - At any point, did reducing the vehicle's cost affect its performance? Describe what you did in this situation.

2. Ask students to describe the **trade-offs,** or compromises, they made when modifying their vehicles on the basis of cost.

3. Have students disassemble their vehicles and return all building pieces to their buckets. You may want to ask students to inventory their pieces before cleaning up.

Extensions

MATHEMATICS

1. Ask students to describe a strategy that would reduce the cost of their vehicles as much as possible while removing the fewest parts. (One strategy is to remove only costly parts.) Ask how effective this strategy might be.

LESSON 13

SCIENCE **MATHEMATICS**

2. Have students think about the standard vehicle they built using the top- and side-view drawings in Lesson 2. Invite them to evaluate the cost of that vehicle and suggest ways to reduce cost. For each suggestion made, have students explain what effect the change would have.

SOCIAL STUDIES

3. Ask students to suggest how the design of a product currently on the market could be changed to reduce cost. How might the changes affect customers' feelings about buying the product? What features could be added to the product to increase its appeal without significantly increasing cost?

SOCIAL STUDIES **ART**

4. Have students collect advertisements that promote products on the basis of their reasonable cost. Students can create their own ads in which cost is the primary selling feature.

SCIENCE

5. Challenge students to design, build, test, and evaluate their own propeller-driven vehicles.

Preparation for Lessons 14 through 16

- Students should have disassembled their vehicles and inventoried the pieces before Lesson 14.

- Students will select from several design challenges in Lesson 14. One of the challenges requires a small electric fan (battery-operated fans do not provide enough airflow) with a protective grill around the blades. The fan creates dramatic results in the design challenge; however, if you cannot obtain a fan, an alternative challenge is provided. Another challenge calls for a "mountain," which can be a piece of Masonite™, foamboard, or other board elevated at one end on a stack of books. Try to obtain both the board and the fan before beginning Lessons 14 through 16.

LESSON 13

Record Sheet 13-A   Names: _____

                                         _____

Date: _____   _____

Evaluating the Cost of Our Design

Building Piece	Cost Per Piece	Number of Pieces Used			Total Cost
Propeller	$500	x		=	
Rods					
Gray	$450	x		=	
Red	$400	x		=	
Yellow	$350	x		=	
White	$300	x		=	
Blue	$250	x		=	
Green	$100	x		=	
Connectors					
White	$250	x		=	
Yellow	$150	x		=	
Green	$150	x		=	
Red	$100	x		=	
Orange	$100	x		=	
Dark gray	$100	x		=	
Brown	$100	x		=	
Wheels					
Small	$200	x		=	
Large	$400	x		=	
Tires					
Small	$100	x		=	
Large	$200	x		=	
				TOTAL	

STC / Motion and Design

LESSON 14

Planning Our Final Design Challenge

Overview and Objectives

Lessons 14 through 16 serve as an embedded assessment that allows students to apply what they have learned about technological design and the physics of motion. In this lesson, students choose from among several design challenges. Teams of six students work cooperatively to decide how they will solve the challenge, design a vehicle, move the vehicle, and test its motion. Through a reading selection, students learn about careers in engineering and recognize how the design skills they have been learning could become part of the work they do as adults.

- Students review roles appropriate for working in cooperative teams.
- Team members independently record and collectively brainstorm possible solutions to a challenge, then select one solution to carry out.
- Teams present their plans to the class for feedback and refinement.
- Through a reading selection, students learn more about engineering as an interest and career.

Background

In this lesson, students work for the first time in teams of six. Combining two groups to solve a design challenge encourages students to analyze and rethink the knowledge they have gained in the past 13 lessons.

Because this is the first time students work in larger groups, you may need to remind them of the importance of cooperative problem solving. Encourage them to share responsibilities by taking on the team roles discussed earlier in the unit. (See Figure 14-1 and the **Background** of Lesson 1 for information on student roles.)

Sometimes the tasks of an engineering project are so specialized that they require the expertise of several different kinds of engineers working as a team. These team members work independently or collectively, as needed. For example, a project to design a satellite might require the following specialists:

- Aerospace engineer—to design a satellite exterior that will withstand the harsh environment of space.
- Computer scientist—to write programs that will control the operation of the satellite.
- Mechanical engineer—to design a system that points the satellite in the right direction.
- Electrical engineer—to design the antennas for communication with earth.

STC / *Motion and Design*

LESSON 14

Like engineers, students have varying strengths in mathematics, art, science, and writing. Remember to consider these strengths when forming teams of six students for this lesson.

Each challenge in this lesson poses a particular problem that demands a multidimensional approach. To solve the challenges, teams devise a vehicle and a system for moving it. Students must refer to previously recorded data as they plan their solutions. By clearly understanding the design process that students have experienced throughout the unit, you can more readily assess your students' skills as they work through this lesson.

Students implemented a technological design process in Lessons 1, 5, and 9 when they took the following steps to meet a design challenge:

- Brainstorm—encourages divergent thinking, which is necessary because there is rarely one solution to a problem.

- Research—helps spark ideas or focus the design through exploration of trade books and other sources.

- Build—complete a product that meets the challenge through use of available tools and materials.

- Test and evaluate—establish whether the final product solves the problem.

- Modify and reevaluate—question and evaluate the product during building and after completion.

Students may have discovered that change does not always mean improvement. Improvement usually comes after many changes. If a vehicle does not meet the design requirements in this lesson, students must decide to which phase of the process they will return—for example, to the initial idea or to an adjustment of the final product.

The following example of the work of the Wright brothers illustrates how engineers use science, math, and a technological design process to solve a practical problem. The example might also help students accept the need to modify their vehicles several times before they meet the requirements.

To build a vehicle that would fly, the Wright brothers overcame many challenges. First, they had to determine the most effective body and wing shape to reduce air resistance. Then they had to construct a strong, light wing and find a lightweight engine. Most difficult of all, they had to discover a way to control the aircraft and achieve stable flight. In 1902, to learn the basic science of air movements and forces, the Wright brothers built a wind tunnel and tested many aircraft models. In more than 1,000 piloted glider flights, they applied their wind tunnel results to controlling and stabilizing a series of gliders. Only when the glider design was successful did the brothers design and build an aircraft powered by a gasoline engine. Orville Wright piloted the craft on its first successful flight at Kitty Hawk, North Carolina, on December 17, 1903.

Materials

For each student
1 science notebook
1 pencil with eraser

For each team of six students
1 copy of **Record Sheet 14-A: Planning Our Final Design Challenge**
1 sheet of newsprint
1 design challenge card

LESSON 14

1 colored marker
1 set of colored pencils
1 circle template
1 metric ruler

For the class

Brainstorming list, "What We Know about the Motion and Design of Vehicles" (from Lesson 1)

Design Challenge Cards: Lesson 14 (blackline master, pgs. 150–52)

1 fine-point, black permanent marker
Assorted colored markers
Masking tape
Scissors

Preparation

1. Display the class brainstorming list from Lesson 1.

2. Decide how you will form teams of six students. The easiest way is to combine two groups, keeping in mind students' different strengths and abilities. (See **Background** of this lesson and Lesson 1 for information on grouping.) Also decide how you will divide the five design challenge cards among the teams so that each challenge goes to at least one team. Teams can select a challenge or you can assign them.

3. Make one copy of **Record Sheet 14-A: Planning Our Final Design Challenge** for each team.

4. Duplicate and cut the **Design Challenge Cards: Lesson 14** (blackline master, pgs. 150–52). You may only need one copy of the blackline master, since each team of six students gets just one design challenge card.

5. Preview each design challenge card. Card A involves the use of an inclined plane—such as a piece of Masonite™ or foamboard, elevated on a stack of books. Card D requires a small electric fan. Both of these tasks will challenge students and produce interesting results. If you are unable to create an incline or obtain the fan, you may need to limit your students' challenges to B, C, and E.

6. Arrange the materials at the distribution center. Students will not need their buckets of building pieces until Lesson 15, when they implement their plans.

Procedure

1. Refer students to the class brainstorming list from Lesson 1. Ask them to discuss which comments on the list they now know to be true. Is there anything on the list they would correct or update? Which investigations in the unit support their ideas?

   Note: This step is a discussion only. You should not write on the brainstorming list from Lesson 1. Students will revisit the list during the post-unit assessments and will record their final changes to the list then.

2. Let students know they will receive a design challenge. They can apply all they have learned up to this point in the unit to respond to this challenge.

3. Divide the class into teams of six. Review the responsibilities of team roles (see Figure 14-1 and the **Background** of Lesson 1). Ask students to spend a few minutes choosing or assigning roles within their teams.

Figure 14-1

Ideas for student jobs

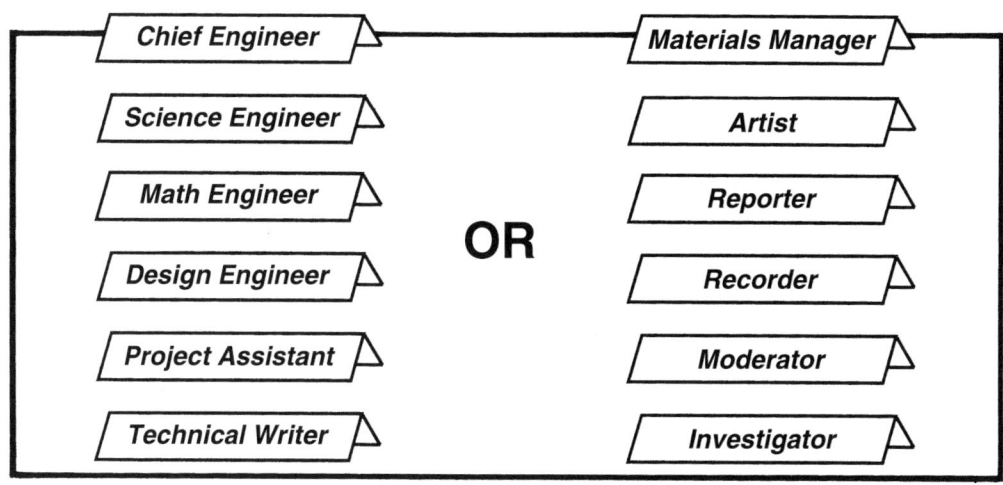

4. Describe the goals and structure of the lesson by reviewing the following steps:

   - Each team receives one design challenge card. Each design challenge requires the team to build a vehicle and design a system for moving it, while meeting a set of requirements.

   - After each team reviews its challenge card, students will *independently* list in their notebooks all the ideas they have for meeting the assigned challenge.

   - Students share their ideas with their team. Using a marker, the team recorder records all the ideas on a sheet of newsprint. Each team displays its list of ideas at the end of this lesson and during a presentation in Lesson 16.

   - Teams use these brainstormed ideas, as well as previously collected data, to plan a solution to the challenge. Teams will record their plan on **Record Sheet 14-A: Planning Our Final Design Challenge.**

   - At the end of the lesson, each team presents its planned solution to the class.

   - Teams will refine and test their solutions in Lesson 15.

   - Teams will present their solutions to the class in Lesson 16.

5. Distribute one design challenge card to each team (or allow teams to select one). Have the reporter from each team read the design challenge aloud to the team. Allow time for clarification of design requirements, if needed.

6. Distribute Record Sheet 14-A. Discuss how teams can plan a solution to their design challenge. Discuss each of the planning points listed on the record sheet. (See Figure 14-2 for an example.)

7. Ask the materials manager from each team to collect a sheet of newsprint, marker, set of colored pencils, ruler, and circle template from the distribution center.

8. Have the reporter from each team label its newsprint "Solutions." Ask students to record independently in their notebooks possible solutions to their design challenges. Then encourage them to brainstorm ideas with their teammates. Have team recorders list all ideas on the newsprint. Make certain each team knows it will need this list for a presentation in Lesson 16.

Figure 14-2

Sample student record sheet

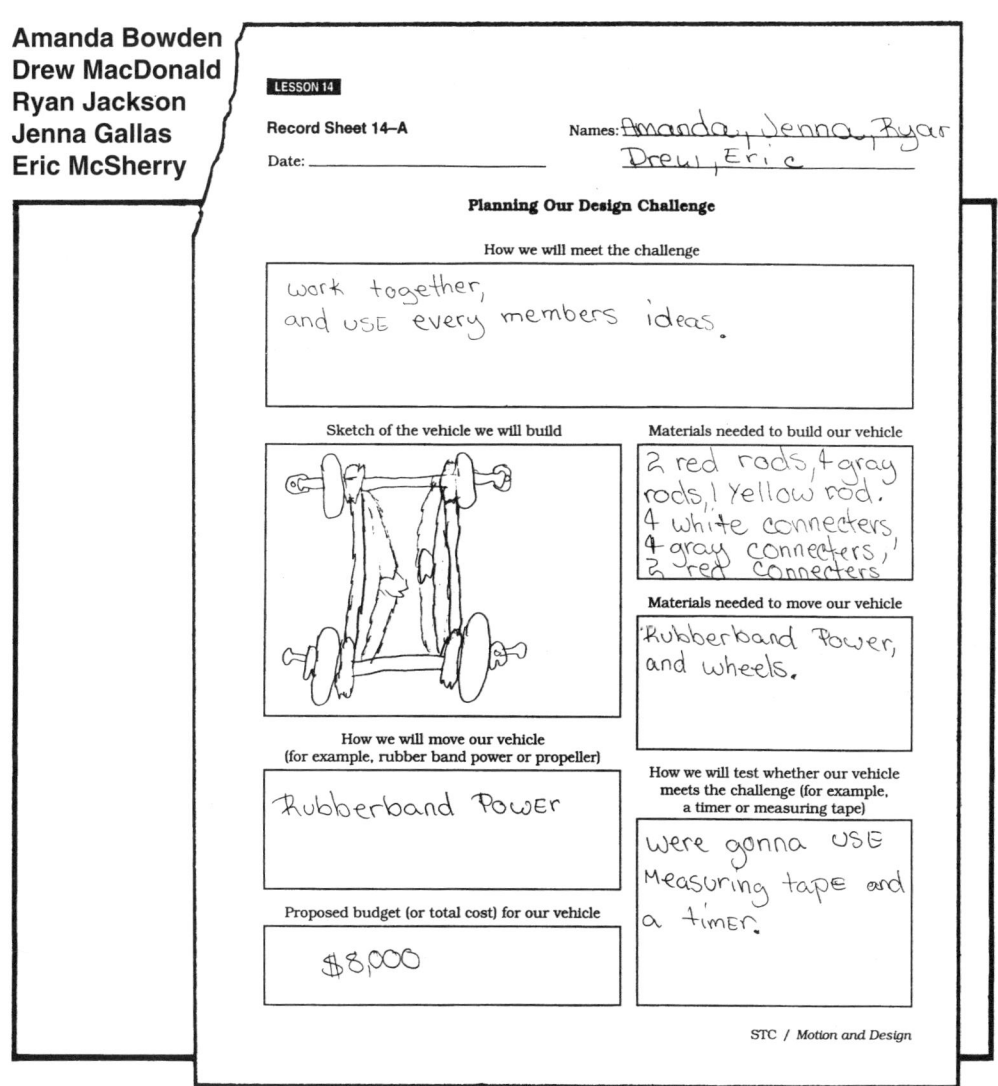

Management Tip: Determine at this point whether each team has a good grasp of how to meet its design challenge. If teams require additional input, you can suggest that they rotate around the room at this time. As each team visits another team's work space, have them read that team's challenge and brainstorming list and then record additional ideas for solving the challenge on the list. When teams return to their own work space, they can read and discuss the suggestions other teams have given them and select the solution they think would work best.

9. Ask teams to consider the lists of solutions they worked out by brainstorming and then to finalize their plan by deciding on one solution. Have students record their plan on the record sheet.

10. Encourage each team to sketch its proposed vehicle and the system for moving it (rubber band, propeller, falling weights). Remind teams to use colored pencils, the circle template, ruler, and graph paper when sketching their designs. Students can tape their planning record sheet and drawings to the team brainstorming list.

LESSON 14

Final Activities

1. Ask teams to display their lists of ideas. Discuss each team's planned solution to its design challenge. Have students share any difficulties they had in developing a team solution to the challenge.

2. Ask teams to display the sketches of their proposed vehicles. Discuss special features of each proposed vehicle and how each feature will help the vehicle meet the challenge.

3. Encourage other teams to offer feedback regarding each team's solution and proposed vehicle.

4. Allow teams to modify their plans and sketches as needed, on the basis of the class feedback. Ask students to record in their notebooks responses to the following questions:

   - What is your team's final solution to the challenge?
   - Why did your team decide on this solution?

5. Have students clean up. They should set aside their brainstorming lists for use in Lessons 15 and 16.

6. Assign the reading selection "Making the Switch from Kids' Stuff to Engineering" (pgs.147–48 in this guide and pgs. 60–61 in the Student Activity Book). Ask students to list in their notebooks activities they do at home or in school that relate to engineering and technological design (designing products, systems, or environments that solve problems and extend human capabilities).

Extensions

SCIENCE

1. Set up an invention area where students can bring in devices developed either by themselves or by others. Have them present the items to the class.

SCIENCE

2. Encourage students to develop design requirements for a product they would like to make with the building pieces. Have them build the product and present it to the class.

SOCIAL STUDIES **LANGUAGE ARTS**

3. Invite students to research an invention and its inventor. Have them identify some qualities of inventors.

Assessment

Lessons 14 through 16 provide an opportunity to assess how well students apply the concepts, skills, and attitudes addressed in the unit. The assessment section at the end of Lesson 16 (see pgs. 165–66) provides a detailed summary of strategies you can use to assess students' work during these three lessons.

Reading Selection

Making the Switch from Kid's Stuff to Engineering

Linda and Juan work as engineers for a big automobile company. They designed many of the cars you see every day on the road. What kinds of things did Linda and Juan like to do when they were kids? How did these interests help them become engineers? Let's find out.

Not Just Playing Around

Linda always enjoyed taking things apart. She liked to see what was inside them. She also liked to put them back together. When her bicycle broke down, she fixed it herself. Her mother and father were amazed. When her parents bought a computer, Linda said "Wow!" She used the computer more often than her parents did. She even bought books to learn how it worked.

Juan liked to play with his chemistry set most of all. Whenever he read a book about chemistry, he got ideas for experiments. Then he would mix together the chemicals and see if his ideas were right. As Juan got older, he also liked to tinker with the family's lawn mower. One spring he said to his father, "Don't take the lawn mower to the shop this year. I will fix it myself." And he did. By reading the manual and checking out different parts, he learned how to keep the mower running just right.

Math and Science Count!

Both Linda and Juan liked math and science in school. They took every math and science class they could. In her physics class, Linda became interested in how forces make objects turn and move. Juan loved chemistry, especially when he learned about how gasoline burns in a car engine.

When Linda and Juan went to college, they already knew from their earlier experiences that they would like to become engineers. They studied more math and science. They also studied how engineers use math and science in their work. After they graduated from college, they landed their first jobs in the same company.

LESSON 14

Remember how Linda liked to work with computers? Well, now she designs the computers inside cars. Juan uses his interest in chemistry when he designs new car engines. They both love their work. Just like when they were kids, they get to tinker and explore every day! And, working together, they make better cars for people to drive.

Are you like Linda and Juan? What math and science activities do you like? What do you think you'd like to be when you grow up?

LESSON 14

Record Sheet 14–A

Names: _____ _____

_____ _____

Date: _____ _____ _____

Planning Our Final Design Challenge

How we will meet the challenge

[   ]

Sketch of the vehicle we will build

[   ]

Materials needed to build our vehicle

[   ]

Materials needed to move our vehicle

[   ]

How we will move our vehicle (for example, rubber band power or falling weight)

[   ]

How we will test whether our vehicle meets the challenge (for example, use a timer or a measuring tape)

[   ]

Proposed budget (or total cost) for our vehicle

[   ]

STC / *Motion and Design*

Blackline Master

Design Challenge Cards: Lesson 14

Challenge A

You are part of a famous engineering design team. An agency just awarded your team a contract to design a rescue vehicle for saving mountain climbers who are trapped at the top of snowcapped mountains. The vehicle you design must move as quickly as possible without causing an avalanche.

Design requirements:

- Your vehicle must move up the hill within five seconds or less.
- Your vehicle must stop moving within 5 cm (2 in) of the top of the hill
- The top of your incline must be at least 20 cm (8 in) off the ground.

Cost is important. You must build the vehicle as inexpensively as possible without affecting its performance.

Challenge B

You are part of a famous engineering design team. An agency just awarded your team a contract to design a vehicle that services a hospital's rooftop heliport (a landing place for helicopters). The vehicle will be used to transport patients slowly from a helicopter to the elevator near the edge of the roof.

Design requirements:

- Your vehicle must move across a table, a squared-off area of the floor, or other area that simulates a rooftop heliport.
- Your vehicle must start in the center of the roof and move toward the edge of the area.
- Your vehicle must be able to move this distance slowly, in three seconds or more.
- Your vehicle must stop within 5 cm (2 in) of the edge.
- Your vehicle must move backward to return to the center of the roof.

Cost is important. You must build the vehicle as inexpensively as possible without affecting its performance.

STC / *Motion and Design*

Blackline Master

Design Challenge Cards: Lesson 14, *continued*

Challenge C

You are part of a famous engineering design team. An agency has just awarded your team a contract to design a pizza delivery truck. To keep the customers happy, the driver of the vehicle must be able to travel quickly and safely both long and short distances and deliver the pizzas piping hot.

Design requirements:

- Your vehicle must be able to carry one load of pizzas (represented by one block).
- Your vehicle must move quickly and safely (in 4 seconds or less).
- Your vehicle must travel at least 3 m (10 ft) and deliver the pizza within 50 cm (20 in) of the 3-m mark.
- Your vehicle must return to the pizza shop (starting line) without its load of pizzas in 7 seconds or less.

Cost is important. You must build the vehicle as inexpensively as possible without affecting its performance.

Challenge D

You are part of a famous engineering design team. An agency has just awarded your team a contract to design a parade float that is powered by air pushing it from behind. The parade float must travel long distances at a slow speed.

Design requirements:

- Your parade float must use a sail to help it move.
- Propelled by a fan, your vehicle must move 3 m (10 ft) in 10 seconds or more.

Cost is important. You must build the vehicle as inexpensively as possible without affecting its performance.

STC / *Motion and Design*

Blackline Master

Design Challenge Cards: Lesson 14, *continued*

Challenge E

You are part of a famous engineering design team. An agency has just awarded your team a contract to design a drag racing car. The dragster must move a relatively short distance as quickly as possible and then come to a stop.

Design requirements:

- In 2 seconds or less, your vehicle must move from the starting line to the finish line.
- The distance of the race track is 2 m (6½ ft).
- Your vehicle must stop within 50 cm (20 in) of the finish line.
- You may drag weights or other objects behind your vehicle to slow it down.

Cost is important. You must build the vehicle as inexpensively as possible without affecting its performance.

LESSON 15

Refining Our Design

Overview and Objectives

Students complete their design process in this lesson by building and testing the vehicles they planned in Lesson 14. Through repeated evaluation, students improve their designs to meet two requirements: high performance and low cost. This lesson sets the stage for Lesson 16, in which students present their challenges to the class and describe ways in which their team met the requirements.

- Students implement their plans from Lesson 14 by building, testing, and evaluating their vehicles and the systems for moving them.

- Students determine the cost of their designs.

Background

In Lesson 14, each team selected a solution to its design challenge and formulated a plan. Most teams will recognize that even with a good plan, they need to be flexible and willing to make changes in the plan as successes or difficulties arise. This is an important skill in meeting design requirements.

You may need to remind students that testing and refining are essential parts of technological design. Test results at one stage supply information for the next stage. Refinement incorporates those results and further improves the design. Engineers repeat the process until the product meets the requirements as inexpensively as possible.

One engineer who repeatedly refined a product was John Holland, the inventor of the modern submarine. Holland immigrated to the United States from Ireland. His first submarine, built in 1878, sank immediately. After reworking the flotation system, he commanded the first successful submarine dive. Then he produced a series of submarines, culminating in 1897 with one that could travel underwater for more than 64 km (40 miles). In just 19 years he had progressed from making the first crude working model to developing a submersible that incorporated almost all of the elements of the modern submarine.

More recently, the invention of the transistor enabled engineers to miniaturize electronic circuits and improve electronic products at an astonishing rate. The speed of computers, which use electronic circuits, has doubled every two years, while cost continues to drop. Satellite dishes grow smaller, and telephones are portable. These product refinements—the result of technological design—have changed the way we live.

LESSON 15

Materials

For each student
- 1 science notebook
- 1 pencil with eraser
- Safety goggles

For each team of six students
- 1 copy of **Record Sheet 14-A: Planning Our Final Design Challenge** (completed in Lesson 14)
- 1 team brainstorming list, "Solutions" (from Lesson 14)
- 2 clean copies of **Record Sheet 13-A: Evaluating the Cost of Our Design**
- 2 buckets of building pieces
- 1 measuring tape, 100 cm (39 in)
- 1 timer
- 1 calculator (optional)

For the class
- 1 spool of light string
- 5 blocks of wood, 5 × 8 × 9 cm (2 × 3 × 3½ in)
- 1 bucket of extra building pieces
- 2 small- to medium-sized electric fans
- 5 pieces of cardboard, 23 × 30 cm (9 × 12 in)
- 4 sets of three connected rubber bands, No. 16
- 4 sets of three connected rubber bands, No. 64
- 4 propeller units
- 5 strips of Masonite™, 38 × 122 × 0.6 cm (15 × 48 × ¼ in), or foamboard, 38 × 122 × 0.5 cm (15 × 48 × 3/16 in) (optional)
- 3 rolls of masking tape
- Books (for creating incline)
- Large paper clips
- Large washers
- Small washers
- Hole punches (optional)

Preparation

1. Make two copies of **Record Sheet 13-A: Evaluating the Cost of Our Design** for each team.

2. Make certain students have appropriate work areas. Some teams will need an elevated work space. Others will want floor space. Arrange for use of cafeteria tables and floor space, if possible.

3. Review each team's plan on **Record Sheet 14-A: Planning Our Final Design Challenge.** Meet with each team to assess whether all members understand the proposed solution to the challenge.

4. Prepare the connected rubber bands. Make certain you have enough sets so that each team that plans to build an axle-driven or a propeller-driven vehicle has one set of large (No. 64) connected rubber bands (three per set) and one set of small (No. 16) connected rubber bands (three per set).

5. Prepare a string with paper clip hooks for each team that plans to use a weighted string to pull its vehicle. Wrap each string around a piece of cardboard to prevent tangling.

6. Assemble the materials at the distribution center as shown in Figure 15-1. Display the materials in separate containers. Because each team requires different materials, use index cards to label the containers "Take as needed for your design."

Figure 15-1

Sample distribution center for planning the design challenge

Procedure

1. Ask students to refer to their "Solutions" list from Lesson 14 and to the completed **Record Sheet 14-A: Planning Our Final Design Challenge.** What materials do they need to build and test their vehicles? Have students pick up their materials.

2. Allow time for students to set up their systems and build, test, evaluate, and refine their vehicle designs on the basis of their plans. Students can add to their "Solutions" sheet a list of ways they have refined, or changed, their vehicles to meet their design requirements, as shown in Figure 15-2.

3. Ask each team to determine the cost of its vehicle by completing **Record Sheet 13-A: Evaluating the Cost of Our Design.** Encourage students to use the second copy of the record sheet if they modify their vehicles to reduce cost. (Remind students that they determined the value for an expensive and inexpensive vehicle in Lesson 13.) Ask teams to retest their vehicles' performance to make certain the modified vehicles still meet the design requirements.

LESSON 15

Figure 15-2

Final results from two teams

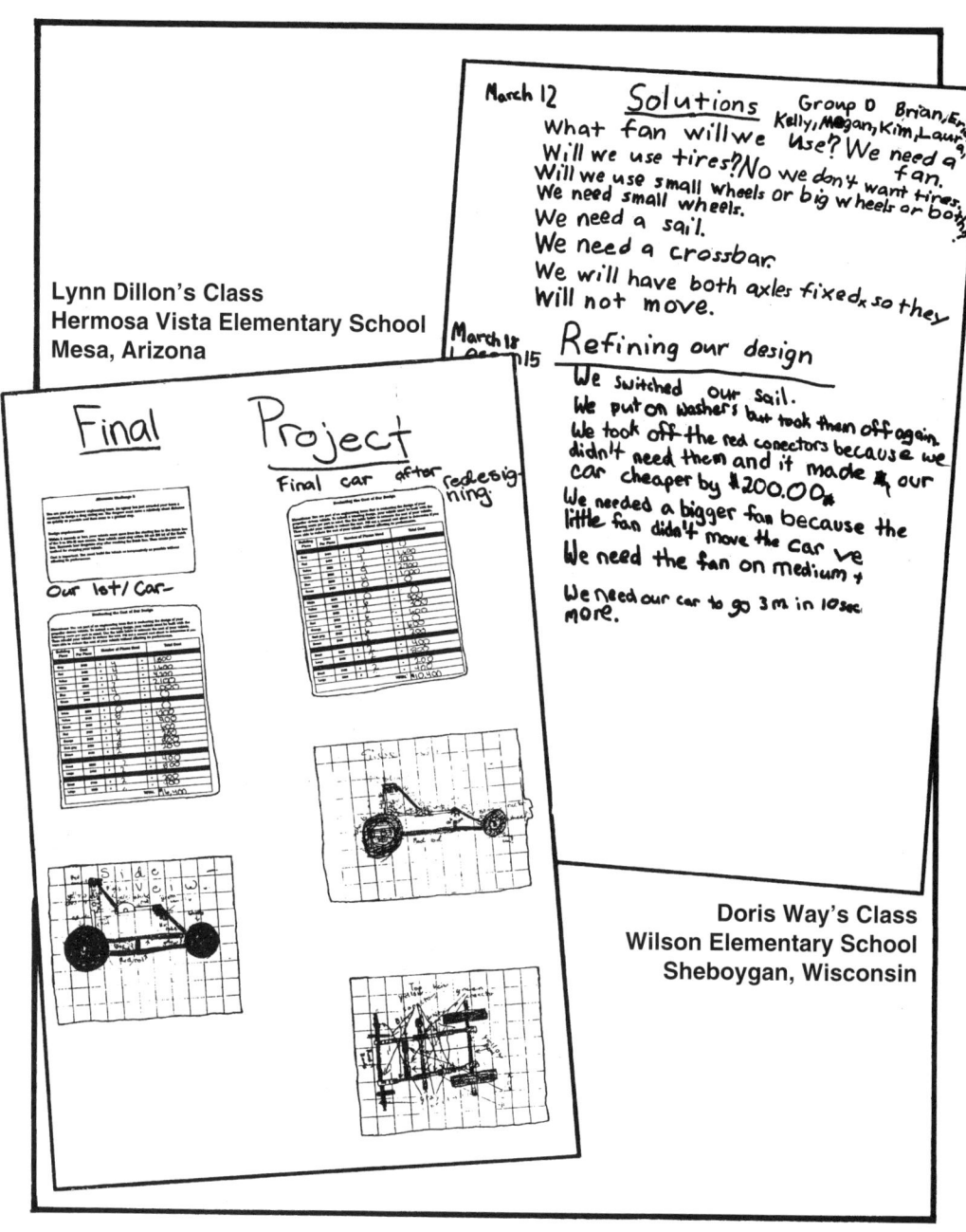

Lynn Dillon's Class	
Hermosa Vista Elementary School	
Mesa, Arizona	

Doris Way's Class
Wilson Elementary School
Sheboygan, Wisconsin

Final Activities

1. Ask teams to label their vehicles and other materials. They will need them in Lesson 16 for their presentations. Have students return their vehicles and other materials to the distribution center.

2. Ask students to suggest how teams could present their solutions in Lesson 16. Possibilities include the following:

   - Invite guests.

   - Use props or backdrops to emphasize the "engineering design team" approach to solving the challenge.

   - Create a story or context for the presentations. For example, students could be part of an engineering team that is making a presentation to a large company.

Extensions

SCIENCE

1. Ask students to select a product and imagine how it will be improved in the future.

SOCIAL STUDIES   **LANGUAGE ARTS**

2. Ask students to research the history of improvements to the television set and report their findings to the class. Students can create a time line describing these changes over time.

LANGUAGE ARTS

3. Ask students to write a story about an inventor who works in the attic each night on a strange new invention.

LANGUAGE ARTS   **SOCIAL STUDIES**

4. Have students develop and perform a skit that shows how the telephone has changed since its invention.

Preparation for Lesson 16

If you plan to invite other classes or family members to view the presentations in Lesson 16, make the necessary preparations. Send out notices or invitations and reserve a room for the presentations.

LESSON 16

Presenting Our Final Design Challenge

Overview and Objectives

In Lessons 14 and 15, students modeled the work of technological design teams by cooperating to solve challenges that simulate real-world situations. In this lesson, students gain experience in oral communication, listening, and leadership skills as they describe to their classmates and others the materials and methods they used to meet their design challenges—a process often used by engineers. Students then reflect on this process and discover its application in daily problem-solving experiences.

- Teams present their solutions to a design challenge.

- Students evaluate each team's solution for meeting the design requirements.

- Students think about their own lives and how they can apply their knowledge of technological design to the world around them.

- Students make a final record of their designs.

Background

After a team of engineers creates a design, they often make a presentation highlighting important product features that fulfill the design requirements. The team might give the presentation for the company's management. Or it might give the presentation for a client who is considering project designs from several companies. This process is often called a preliminary design review, critical design review, or system design review. On the basis of these presentations or reviews, the client identifies a preferred design and selects the company to build it.

Like a team of engineers, students in this lesson make presentations in which they describe the methods they used to solve the design challenge given to them in Lessons 14 and 15. Students in the audience can ask a team about its initial plan and how they modified and refined the vehicle while building it. The team may also want to speculate on how it could further refine the vehicle.

This culminating activity should be an enjoyable experience. Help students feel successful in their accomplishments. Encourage them to focus on the presentation as a way to explore what worked and did not work in their plans. Even teams that feel they did not solve their design challenge are successful if they planned and attempted to implement a solution. Allow those individuals or teams that feel uncomfortable making a class presentation to serve as a "management team" or "review panel" to oversee the details of accommodating guests and facilitating the team presentations.

LESSON 16

Materials

For each student
- 1 science notebook
- Safety goggles

For each team of six students
- 1 vehicle and system for moving it (from Lesson 15)
- 1 team brainstorming list, "Solutions" (from Lesson 14)
- Costumes and props to enhance presentation
- 2 sets of colored pencils
- 2 circle templates
- 2 metric rulers
- 2 buckets of building pieces

For the class
- Masking tape

Preparation

1. Arrange the room to accommodate team presentations. Make certain that an elevated work space is available for teams that need one.
2. Prepare seating for any invited guests.
3. Arrange the materials at the distribution center, if needed.

Procedure

1. Before asking teams to begin their presentations, remind students in the audience to ask questions at the end of each presentation (see Background for more information).

Figure 16-1

Making a presentation

2. Have each team present its design challenge and solution by demonstrating the motion of its vehicle. Remind students to display their team brainstorming list from Lesson 14, sketches of their vehicle designs, cost sheets, and other design records. Encourage teams to describe in detail how they met their design challenges. Some teams may decide to use props or costumes for their presentations.

Management Tip: You can use the presentations to assess each student's knowledge of motion and design concepts, skill at manipulating the materials, and attitudes. Use the questions listed in the **Assessment** at the end of this lesson (pgs. 165–66) as a guide. You may wish to take notes during the presentations.

Figure 16-2

One teacher's assessment notes

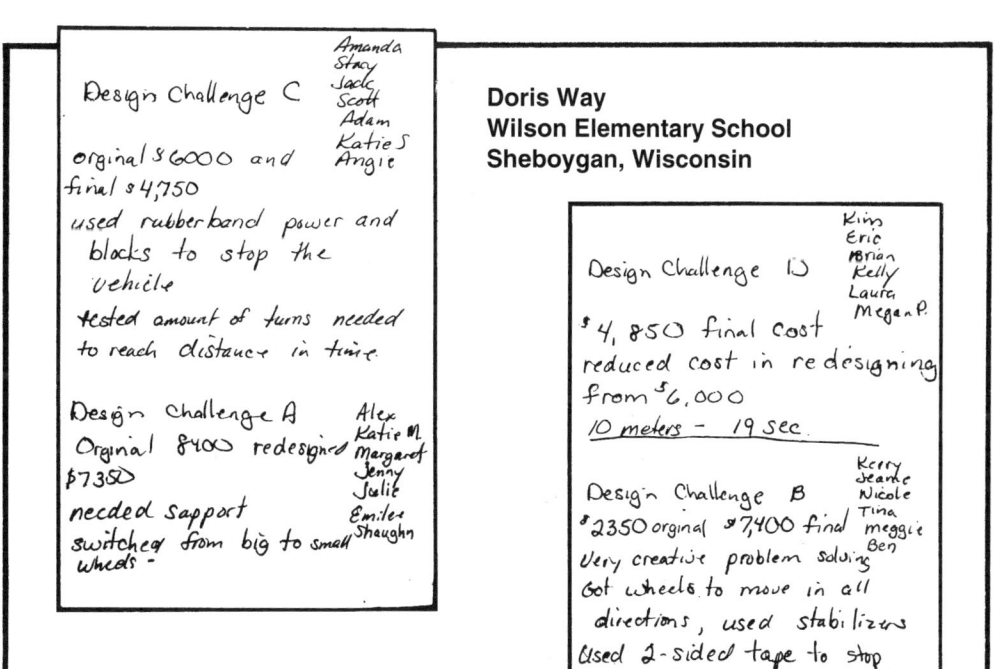

3. Have students discuss the presentations. Encourage members of the presenting team to describe what they would do differently, given another chance to solve the challenge.

Final Activities

1. Have students collect from the distribution center their buckets of building pieces and the tools needed to make a final record of their vehicle (circle template, ruler, and colored pencils) (see Figure 16-3).

2. After students have drawn their vehicles, ask them to disassemble the vehicles and return all building pieces to their buckets. Ask students to inventory their pieces before returning all materials to the distribution center.

3. Bring the unit to a close with a reflective writing activity. Have students respond in their notebooks to one or more of the following topics:

   ■ Describe the steps you used in solving design challenges throughout this unit.

LESSON 16

Figure 16-3

One team's technical drawing

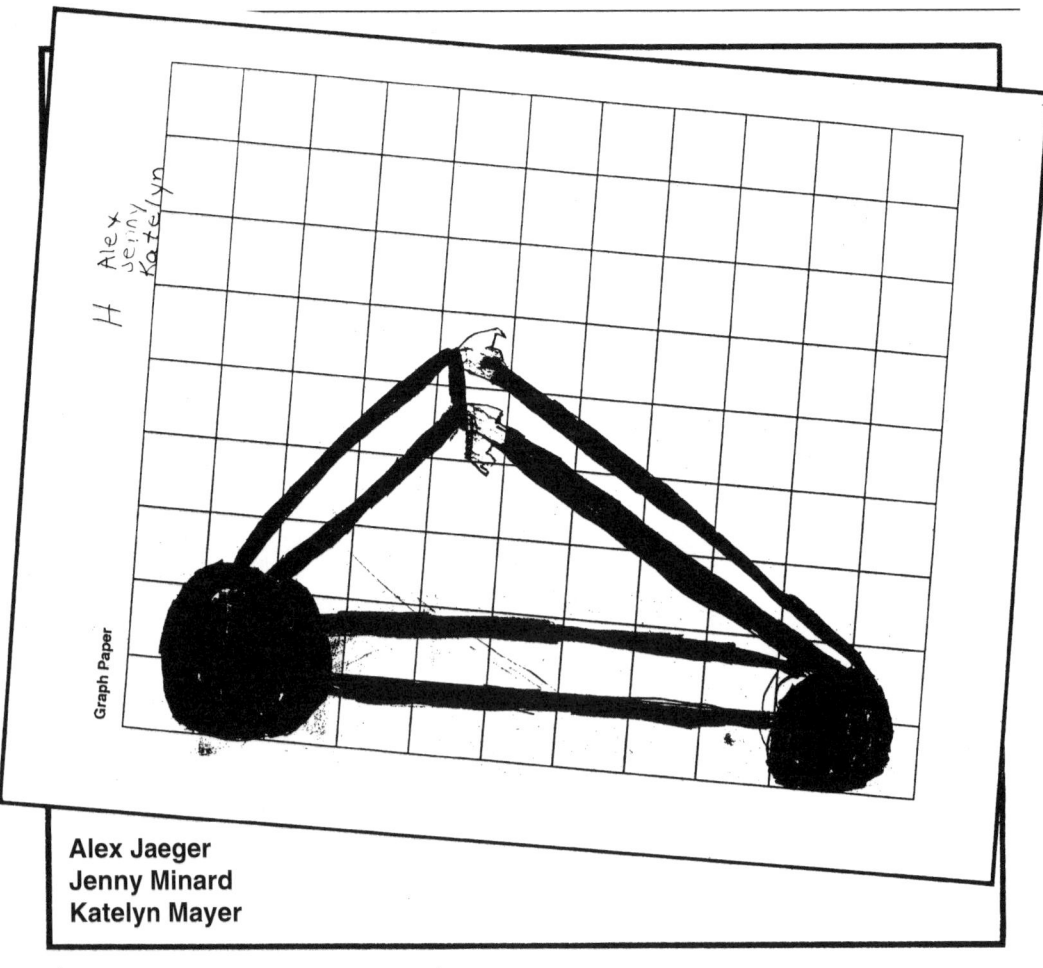

Alex Jaeger
Jenny Minard
Katelyn Mayer

- Describe how your vehicle moved and what method you used to move it.
- Describe something you do at home or in school in which you use problem-solving skills like those in this unit.
- Describe how you might use the steps of technological design in making a paper airplane or building a sand castle.
- Describe one product that has changed greatly over the years. Why were these changes made? Do you feel the changes were good ones?
- Describe the similarities and differences between what happened in the classroom in the last three lessons and what engineering teams or scientists do to solve a problem.

4. Have students share their ideas.

Extensions

SCIENCE

1. Have students identify a need that could be met by an invention. Invite them to plan the invention, build it, and present it to the class.

SCIENCE

2. Ask students to identify activities they do outside of school in which they use the steps of technological design. Examples include designing a game to play with a friend or fixing a broken bicycle chain.

Assessment

Lessons 14 through 16 provide an opportunity to assess how well students can build, test, modify, and retest. Useful information includes student notebook entries, brainstorming lists, and the vehicle built by each team. The reflective writing completed at the end of this lesson is a good opportunity for you to analyze to what extent each student can apply knowledge of motion and design gained in this unit to his or her daily life. Keep the following questions in mind as you assess each student's progress:

Class Discussion

- How well does the student describe the process that led to the solution? Can he or she clearly express how making decisions helped in meeting the design requirements?
- How does the student present test results? Is there enough detail?
- If the team removed parts to reduce cost, can the student describe how that removal affected performance?

Vehicle

- How does the vehicle incorporate what the student has learned throughout the unit?
- How did the student ensure that the wheels spin freely? Did the team make the frame strong enough?

As you examine the student work products and discuss the results from this lesson with students, try to evaluate how well they understand the technological design process. Why did they make a particular change? How did a test result prompt them to modify the vehicle? Was the modification an improvement? If students can state their answers in this context, they have made great progress in technological design.

Initial Plan

- How did the plan convey what the team was trying to do? Did the student use drawings?
- In what ways do the drawings provide important detail?
- Did the student record why the team approached the design challenge as it did?

Building and Testing the Vehicle

- How did the student contribute to the team's building of the vehicle?
- How well did the student work with the team when testing the vehicle?
- Can the student describe how the team met the design requirements?
- How well did the student implement his or her knowledge of motion in testing the vehicle?

Making a Record of the Vehicle

- During the presentation, how did the student describe the team's vehicle?
- How did the student use drawings to provide information about the vehicle? Do the drawings use color or labels?
- Do the drawings show the vehicle from a particular perspective? Did the student use enough different views to show how the vehicle was made?

LESSON 16

Post-Unit Assessment

The post-unit assessment (pgs. 169–71) is a matched follow-up to the pre-unit assessment in Lesson 1. By comparing students' pre- and post-unit responses, you can document their growth in knowledge about motion and design.

Additional Assessments

The additional assessments (pgs. 173–84) include a self-assessment for students similar to the one they completed in Lesson 9, as well as other means for you to assess their progress.

Post-Unit Assessment

Overview

This post-unit assessment is matched to the pre-unit assessment in Lesson 1. By comparing individual and class responses to activities in this assessment with those from Lesson 1, you can document each student's learning over the course of the unit. In Lesson 1, students developed two lists: "What We Know about the Motion and Design of Vehicles" and "What We Want to Find Out about Motion and Design." They also designed, built, and tested their own vehicle on the basis of a set of requirements. As students revisit the class brainstorming lists and the records of the vehicle they made in Lesson 1 and compare them with those in this activity, they might realize how much they have learned about technological design and the relationships between force and motion.

Materials

For each student
- 1 science notebook (with entries from Lesson 1 and drawing from Lesson 2)
- 1 pencil with eraser
  Safety goggles

For each group of three students
- 1 bucket of building pieces (see blackline master **Building Pieces for Each Group,** pg. 28)

For the class
- 2 class brainstorming lists, "What We Know about the Motion and Design of Vehicles" and "What We Want to Find Out about Motion and Design" (from Lesson 1)
- 1 sheet of newsprint
- 1 spool of light string
  Cardboard sails, 23 × 30 cm (9 × 12 in)
  Small rubber bands, No. 16
  Large rubber bands, No. 64
  Propeller units (includes propeller, screw hook, brass eyelets, and white connector)
  Strips of Masonite™, 38 × 122 × 0.6 cm (15 × 48 × ¼ in), or foamboard, 38 × 122 × 0.5 cm (15 × 48 × 3/16 in) (optional)
  Colored pencils
  Circle templates

Metric rulers
Measuring tapes, 100 cm (39 in)
Graph paper
Jumbo paper clips
Large washers
Small washers
Scissors
Assorted colored markers
Masking tape
Books (for elevating runway)

Preparation

1. Label the new sheet of newsprint with the following title: "What We Now Know about the Motion and Design of Vehicles." Date and hang the newsprint.

2. Have on hand for comparison the class brainstorming lists from Lesson 1, "What We Know about the Motion and Design of Vehicles" and "What We Want to Find Out about Motion and Design." Set out markers of a different color next to each list. Using the markers, date each list.

3. Make certain each group's bucket of building pieces is complete. If not, refer to the blackline master **Building Pieces for Each Group** (pg. 28), and have student volunteers replenish the sets, as needed.

4. Arrange all materials at the distribution center. Students will pick up their buckets and select materials for their investigation.

Procedure

1. Explain that students will revisit some questions they discussed in the first lesson and throughout the unit. Draw students' attention to the new brainstorming list. Ask them to date a clean sheet of paper in their notebooks and to write what they now know about designing vehicles and how vehicles move.

2. Have students share their ideas. Record them on the newsprint labeled "What We Now Know about the Motion and Design of Vehicles."

3. Display the brainstorming list from Lesson 1 titled "What We Know about the Motion and Design of Vehicles." Encourage students to compare information recorded in this lesson with information on the list from Lesson 1. Ask students to identify statements on the list from Lesson 1 that they now know to be true. What experiences did they have during the unit that confirmed these statements? Ask students to identify statements on the list from Lesson 1 that they would like to change. Again, have them support their conclusions with evidence or experiences from the unit. Record their ideas on the original list using a marker of a different color.

4. Divide the class into the original groups of three. Have each group sit together.

5. Present the design challenge. Each group must design a vehicle that will move at least 100 cm (39 in). Students can decide how to move the vehicle and what materials are needed to build it. Have groups discuss possible designs. Ask students to spend a few minutes sketching in their notebooks the design for their group's proposed vehicle.

6. Ask each group to pick up its bucket of building pieces from the distribution center and any other materials they may need to complete the design challenge.

7. Allow students time to build, test, evaluate, and modify their vehicles. When they are testing, have groups record in their notebooks a description of the motion of their vehicles. Groups should also draw their vehicle using the circle template, ruler, and colored pencils.

8. Invite students to share with the class, you, or another group how they met the design requirement.

9. Review with students the class list "What We Want to Find Out about Motion and Design" from Lesson 1. Have them identify the questions they can now answer. Record their answers on the list. Ask students how they could find answers to other questions they are still unable to answer. Encourage them to research and continue looking for answers to these questions.

10. When you assess each student's progress by comparing the pre- and post-unit brainstorming lists (see Figure P-1) and individual student responses, look for evidence to answer the following questions:

   ■ Does the student understand that a variety of forces (push or pull) can move objects and that different forces produce different effects on a vehicle's motion?

   ■ How does the student demonstrate his or her knowledge of the technological design process? How does the student meet design requirements?

   ■ Is the student now more aware that force affects motion? In what ways does he or she demonstrate this knowledge?

   ■ How does the student demonstrate that energy stored in a rubber band can be used to move a vehicle?

Figure P-1

Sample of matched pre- and post-unit class lists

11. When reviewing student notebook entries and work products for this assessment, consider the following questions:
    - In what ways is the vehicle built by the student's group in this assessment different from that in Lesson 1?
    - Does the student and group choose to move the vehicle in a way different from the vehicle in Lesson 1?
    - When building the vehicle, does the student apply an understanding that friction affects motion?
    - Can the student describe the motion of the vehicle and the reason for its motion?
    - How have the student's sketches and final design records changed since Lesson 2? Does the student readily use drawing tools to make the records clear?

Additional Assessments

Overview

The following four assessment activities can provide additional information about student learning. It is not essential to do all these activities. Using different kinds of assessments allows students with different learning styles to express their knowledge and skills. Select assessments that you think will be helpful for evaluating student learning.

- **Assessment 1** is a second self-assessment that students can use to monitor their own learning.

- **Assessment 2** is a performance-based assessment that enables you to assess, while students are working, their conceptual knowledge of motion and their skill in designing and building a vehicle.

- **Assessment 3** enables you to assess students' ability to apply their learning from the unit to a new situation. Students evaluate the designs of real-world vehicles for their function and performance.

- **Assessment 4** asks students to reflect on their work throughout the unit by creating a portfolio in which they place work products that are representative of their learning.

Assessment 1: Student Self-Assessment

This self-assessment, which matches the assessment in Lesson 9, encourages students to evaluate their own progress. By doing the assessment a second time, students can compare their earlier and later responses and get a picture of their growth.

Teachers have found it useful to meet with each student individually to discuss these self-assessments. Such meetings give the teacher the opportunity to provide feedback about the student's work and to compare it with the student's perceptions.

Materials

For each student
1 copy of **Student Self-Assessment A** (completed in Lesson 9)
1 copy of **Student Self-Assessment B**
1 pencil with eraser

Preparation Make one copy of Student Self-Assessment B (pgs. 180–81 in this guide) for each student.

Procedure
1. Distribute **Student Self-Assessment B** to each student. Explain that the assessment allows students to think about their work during the unit, just as they did in Lesson 9.
2. Allow students time to complete the assessment in class.
3. Return **Student Self-Assessment A** to students, if you collected it, or ask students to take it from their notebooks. Invite students to compare Assessment B with Assessment A. To help them compare, have students respond to the following questions in their notebooks:
   - In which areas do you think you showed the most growth?
   - How have your feelings about working with your group members changed?

Assessment 2: And They're Off!

This assessment enables students to apply what they have learned about motion and design to a new design challenge—building a vehicle for racing. It allows you to assess students' conceptual knowledge of motion and their skill in building while they design and race a vehicle.

Materials

For each student
- 1 science notebook (with graph paper)
- 1 pencil with eraser

For each team of six
- 2 buckets of building pieces
- 1 measuring tape, 100 cm (39 in)

For the class
- 1 copy of **Building Pieces for Each Group** (blackline master, pg. 28)
- 1 spool of light string
- 1 box of jumbo paper clips
- Large washers
- Small washers
- Small rubber bands, No. 16
- Large rubber bands, No. 64
- Propeller units (includes propeller, screw hook, brass eyelets, and connector)
- Strips of Masonite™, 38 × 122 × 0.6 cm (15 × 48 × ¼ in), or foamboard, 38 × 122 × 0.5 cm (15 × 48 × 3/16 in) (optional)
- Scissors
- Masking tape
- Circle templates
- Metric rulers
- Colored pencils
- Assorted colored markers
- Index cards

Figure AA-1

Sample Student
Self-Assessments
A and B

Sara Rose Gardner

Blackline Master
Motion and Design
Student Self-Assessment A
LESSON 9

Name: Sara R. Gardner
Date: Feb. 20, 1996

1. Write down two or three things you have learned so far from doing the Motion and Design unit that you think are important.

   I learned that there was a vehicle on the moon called the Lunar Rover? I also learned that there was a drag racer named Shirley.

2. How well do you think you and your partners are working together? Give some examples.

   My partner some times gets mad at me when I do something wrong, but we are okay together.

3. How do you feel about working with the materials in the unit? Are your feelings changing as you work through the unit? Give examples.

   I like working with the materials. My feelings change alot. like when I didn't have an ideal to put the sail up. I got really confused.

4. Write down some activities in the unit you have enjoyed. Explain why you liked them.

   I like unit lesson 6 & 9. The reason why I like lesson 6 is because it was fun to do + I liked to wind up the vehicle and let it go.

5. Are there any activities so far in the unit that were confusing or hard to understand? Explain your answer.

   Yes there was a hard + confusing part in this unit. It was the part where we had to put together our own vehicles because the pieces wouldn't do the things I wanted to do.

6. Look at your record sheets and your science notebook. Describe how well you think you recorded your observations and ideas.

   I think I recorded my observations and ideals pretty good.

7. How well do you think you used the materials to meet each of the design challenges?

   Not so well because the design challenges were very, very hard.

8. Think about the work you have done so far in this unit. What do you think you have done very well?

   The thing I have done a good thing on is making designs on graph paper.

   What area of your work do you think you could improve on?

   The area I think I could improve on is making the cars do the right thing.

9. How do you feel about science now? Circle the words that apply to you.

   (a. Interested) b. Relaxed c. Nervous (d. Excited)
   e. Bored f. Confused g. Successful h. Happy
   i. Write down one word of your own okay

STC / Motion and Design

Blackline Master
Motion and Design
Student Self-Assessment B

Name: Sara
Date:

1. Write down two or three things you have learned from doing the Motion and Design unit that you think are important.

   I've learned that all cars need frames and crossbars.

2. How well do you think you and your partners worked together? Give some examples.

   I think we work together really good and did what we were sapose to do.

3. How did you feel about working with the materials in the unit? Did your feelings change as you worked through the unit? Give examples.

   I felt okay working with the materials. My feelings changed a bit through the unit.

4. Write down some activities in the unit you enjoyed. Explain why you liked them.

   I like the rubber-band power vehicle unit because it was fun trying to get it to work and trying to get it to get going and how fast it went.

5. Were there any activities in the unit that you did not understand or that confused you? Explain your answer.

   Yes, there was one. It was the propeller-driven vehicle because we had trable putting on the propeller.

6. Look at your record sheets, your vehicle, and your science notebook. Describe how well you think you recorded your observations and ideas.

   Well, I think I recorded all my observations and ideals pretty good.

7. How well do you think you used the materials to meet each of the design challenges?

   We use the materals well to meet each of the design challenges.

8. Think about the work you did in the unit. What do you think you did very well?

   I think I did well in the Challenge and in Rubber-Band Power, too.

   What area of your work could you improve on?

   The area I could improve on is Propeller-Driven vehicle because it was confuseing on how to put on the propellers.

9. How do you feel about science now? Circle the words that apply to you.

   (a. Interested) (b. Relaxed) c. Nervous (d. Excited)
   e. Bored f. Confused (g. Successful) (h. Happy)
   i. Write down one word of your own

STC / Motion and Design

Preparation

1. Decide how you will divide the class into teams of two or three students.

2. You will need one "race station" for every *two* teams of students. Because there are three kinds of race stations (falling weight, rubber band, and propeller), you will probably need to set up duplicate stations. Each falling-weight race station requires an elevated work space—either a long table or a foamboard runway placed over two desks. The rubber band and propeller race stations can use a large floor area.

3. Arrange the following materials at the race stations:

   - Falling-weight race station—small and large metal washers, string, paper clips, scissors, and two buckets of building pieces.

   - Rubber band axle-driven race station—at least six small rubber bands (connected in sets of three) and two buckets of building pieces.

   - Propeller race station—two propeller units, at least six large rubber bands (connected in sets of three), and two buckets of building pieces.

4. Use a marker and index cards or other heavy paper to make a sign for each race station.

5. Set out the rolls of masking tape in a designated area. Groups will use the tape to make start and finish lines.

Procedure

1. Ask students to share what they know about races and fast-moving vehicles.

2. Divide the students into teams of two or three. Let students know they will be racing vehicles at race stations set up around the room. Before they can race, each team must design and build a vehicle appropriate for that station that will move as fast as possible to win the race. Students should sketch their designs before building.

3. Provide teams with the following guidelines:

   - The two teams at each station should work cooperatively to decide on start and finish lines. Masking tape is available if needed.

   - Teams should work cooperatively to determine requirements for winning the race.

   - Teams may repeat the race as many times as possible in the time available.

   - Between races, teams may give their vehicles "pit stops." During this time, they can adjust their vehicle designs to improve performance during the next race.

4. Ask two teams to go to each race station and begin designing and building their vehicles using the materials available at the race station. When teams complete their vehicles, they can begin their races.

5. As teams work at the race stations, you can circulate around the room to assess students' knowledge about motion and design. Track student progress by taking notes on index cards about the performance of each student (using questions such as the following as a guide), by creating a checklist of concepts and skills you want to assess for each student (see pgs. 10–14 for goals of this unit), or by doing both.

   - Was the student, with his or her team, able to decide on start and finish lines?

   - What special design features did the student suggest to make the vehicle move fast?

- How did the student use past data to make design decisions about the vehicle?
- How did the student use materials at the race station to move the vehicle?
- What changes did the student make to the vehicle, with his or her team, after the first race? Can the student explain why?
- Does the student understand why the winning vehicle in each race was successful?

6. Allow teams to rotate around the room and race at other stations. Students can race their own vehicles or the vehicles that were built for a particular station.

7. Have students clean up. Ask them to disassemble their vehicles and place all building pieces in their buckets. Have students use the blackline master **Building Pieces for Each Group** to inventory the pieces.

Assessment 3: Looking at Real-World Vehicles

This assessment challenges students to apply what they have learned about vehicle design and motion to an evaluation of the design and function of real-world vehicles. Students can complete this assessment, which involves brainstorming and decision making, independently in their notebooks or collectively in groups.

Materials

For each student
1 science notebook
1 pencil with eraser

For each group of three students (or each student)
1 copy of **Seaplane** (blackline master photograph, pg. 182)
1 copy of **Lunar Rover** (blackline master photograph, pg. 183)
1 copy of **1924 Waterloo Boy Tractor** (blackline master photograph, pg. 184)

Preparation

1. Make one copy of each blackline master photograph for each group (or student).

2. Preview the procedures. Depending on how you plan to assess your students, decide if you want them to complete their evaluations independently or to discuss each vehicle first with the group and then record their ideas independently.

Procedure

1. Ask students to brainstorm independently in their notebooks, then as a class, as many different vehicles as possible. Have students describe what each vehicle's function might be, how the design features help it perform that function, and how the design and function might be different from other vehicles they listed in their notebooks. One way to record their ideas is to create a concept web on the chalkboard with the word VEHICLES in the center of the web, as shown in Figure AA-2. (See **Teaching Motion and Design,** pg. 7, for information on webbing.)

2. Distribute copies of the three photographs to each group. Let students know they will apply what they know about vehicle design and performance to real vehicles.

Figure AA-2

Webbing ideas

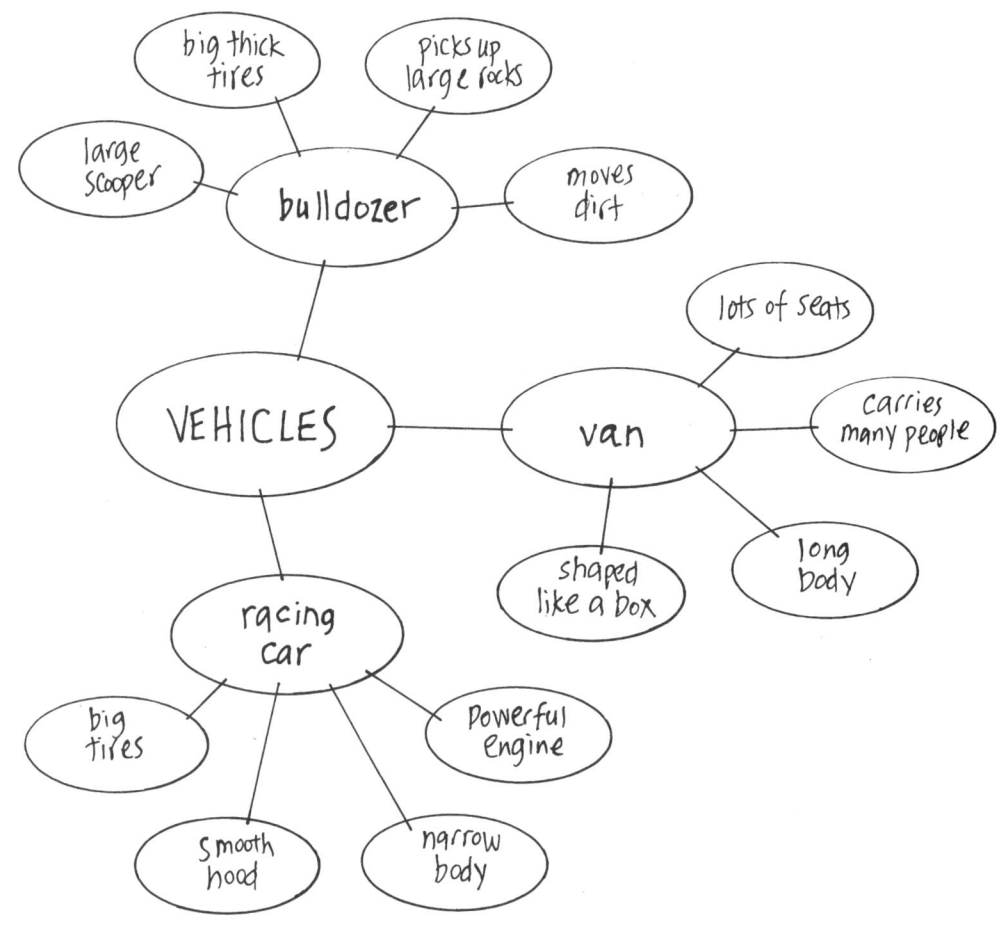

3. Allow groups time to discuss the function of each vehicle, including how the design features help it perform its job. Have students record this information in their notebooks. Encourage them to organize their information in a table, web, or other form of display.

4. Assess how well each student applies information about vehicle design and performance by considering the following questions.

Group Discussion

- How varied were the student's written and verbal lists of vehicles?
- Could the student describe the function of each vehicle and how its design helped its function?
- Could the student recognize differences among vehicles? How specific or general were these noted differences?

Individual Records

- When evaluating the photographs, which design features did the student recognize as being unique to that vehicle?
- Did the student recognize a single, simple function of the vehicle (to move over rough terrain) or more complex functions that related to a design feature (thick tires to move over the Moon's crater-filled surface, or a lightweight frame that enables a rocket to lift the Lunar Rover from Earth without using too much fuel)?

- How did the student express that the vehicle's design helped meet its function?
- Did the student address how the vehicle moved (slowly, by air) and what moved it (propeller, gasoline, solar energy)?
- How did the student organize the information to convey an evaluation of each vehicle? For example, did the student create a table displaying the vehicle's name, design features, and function of each design feature?

Assessment 4: Creating a Portfolio

Throughout the unit, students have kept records of their work. Work products may include notebook entries, record sheets, paper strips with collected data, technical drawings, mathematical tables and graphs from lesson **Extensions**, and photographs that you may have taken of their vehicles in each lesson. A **portfolio** is a selection of materials that represents a student's work throughout the unit. Consider the following guidelines for creating portfolios that you can use to assess students' work:

- Decide who will set the criteria for selecting work to be included in the portfolios (teacher, students, or teacher with input from students).

- Decide who will select the work for the portfolio (teacher, student, or teacher and student).

- List the criteria for selecting work to be included in the portfolio. Decide if the criteria will be specific to the unit (for example, a student's best labeled technical drawing, a photograph of the most elaborate vehicle design, and a data strip with the most accurate predictions), general (for example, a work product that was most difficult to complete or one that the student learned the most from doing), or both specific and general.

- Decide how students will reflect on what has been placed in the portfolio. One kind of reflection involves asking students to explain in writing why they have made a particular selection or why they think you chose a particular selection. Students can also orally reflect on their work by participating in a teacher-student or student-student interview.

- Ask students to include in their portfolio a reflective writing in which they describe their feelings about the unit. Questions they can answer include the following: What have you done in the unit? What have you learned? What did you like best about the unit? What was most difficult about the unit? What would you change if you were to do the unit again? Or students can include their own copies of **Student Self-Assessments A** and **B.**

Blackline Master

Motion and Design
Student Self-Assessment B

Name: _____

Date: _____

1. Write down two or three things you have learned from doing the *Motion and Design* unit that you think are important.

   _____
   _____
   _____

2. How well do you think you and your partners worked together? Give some examples.

   _____
   _____
   _____

3. How did you feel about working with the materials in the unit? Did your feelings change as you worked through the unit? Give examples.

   _____
   _____
   _____

4. Write down some activities in the unit you enjoyed. Explain why you liked them.

   _____
   _____
   _____

5. Were there any activities in the unit that you did not understand or that confused you? Explain your answer.

   _____
   _____
   _____

STC / *Motion and Design*

Blackline Master

Motion and Design
Student Self-Assessment B, *continued*

Name: _____

6. Look at your record sheets and your science notebook. Describe how well you think you recorded your observations and ideas.

   _____
   _____
   _____

7. How well do you think you used the materials to meet each of the design challenges?

   _____
   _____
   _____

8. Think about the work you did in the unit. What do you think you did very well?

   _____
   _____
   _____

   In what area of your work do you think you could improve?

   _____
   _____
   _____

9. How do you feel about science now? Circle the words that apply to you.

   a. Interested   b. Relaxed   c. Nervous   d. Excited

   e. Bored   f. Confused   g. Successful   h. Happy

   i. Write down one word of your own _____

STC / *Motion and Design*

Blackline Master

Seaplane

STC / *Motion and Design*

Blackline Master

Lunar Rover

Photo: Dane Penland. Courtesy of National Air and Space Museum, Smithsonian Institution.

STC / *Motion and Design*

Blackline Master

Waterloo Boy Tractor

STC / *Motion and Design*

Bibliography: Resources for Teachers and Students

This Bibliography provides a sampling of books that complement the *Motion and Design* unit. It is divided into the following categories:

- Resources for Teachers
- Resources for Students

    Physical Science

    Technology, Engineering, and Design

    Inventors and Inventions

    Computer Software and Videocassettes

These materials come well recommended. They have been favorably reviewed, and teachers have found them useful.

If a book goes out of print or if you seek additional titles, you may wish to consult the following resources.

Appraisal: Science Books for Young People (The Children's Science Book Review Committee, Boston).

> Published quarterly, this periodical reviews new science books available for young people. Each book is reviewed by a librarian and by a scientist. The Children's Science Book Review Committee is sponsored by the Science Education Department of Boston University's School of Education and the New England Roundtable of Children's Librarians.

Gath, Tracy, and Maria Sosa, eds. *Science Books & Films' Best Books for Children, 1992–1995*. Washington, DC: American Association for the Advancement of Science, 1996.

> This volume, part of a continuing series, is a compilation of the most highly rated science books that have been reviewed recently in the periodical *Science Books & Films*.

National Science Resources Center. *Resources for Teaching Elementary School Science*. Washington, DC: National Academy Press, 1996.

> This guide provides extensive information about some 350 hands-on, inquiry-centered science curriculum materials for grades K–6. It also annotates other published materials—books on teaching science, science book lists, and periodicals for teachers and students. The guide includes

annotated listings of museums and federal and professional organizations throughout the country with programs and other resources to assist in the teaching of elementary school science.

Science and Children (National Science Teachers Association, Arlington, VA).

Each March, this monthly periodical provides an annotated bibliography of outstanding science trade books primarily aimed at elementary students.

Science Books & Films (American Association for the Advancement of Science, Washington, DC).

Published nine times a year, this periodical offers critical reviews of a wide range of new science materials, from books to audiovisual materials to electronic resources. The reviews are primarily written by scientists and science educators. *Science Books & Films* is useful for librarians, media specialists, curriculum supervisors, science teachers, and others responsible for recommending and purchasing scientific materials.

Scientific American (Scientific American, Inc., New York).

Each December in this monthly periodical, Philip and Phylis Morrison compile and review a selection of outstanding new science books for children.

Resources for Teachers

Bindon, Annette, and Peter Cole. *Teaching Design & Technology in the Primary Classroom.* Walton-on-Thames, Surrey, England: Thomas Nelson, 1992.

Written for primary teachers, this book provides a basis on which to develop strategies for integrating design and technology into the classroom. It is also a resource for solving technological problems that arise as children work. Annotated drawings on various themes, including boats, kites, and building-site machinery, provide ideas for activities.

Chapman, Colin, Val Charles, Mike Finney, Michael Horsley, Heather Jeffrey, and Malcolm Moyes. *Design Technology: Techniques and Resources.* London: Collins Educational, 1993.

This volume contains tips to help elementary teachers and students make things and information to help teachers better understand design technology. It focuses on food, textiles, clay, wood, metal, plastic, paper, and cards and the tools needed to use these materials.

Dishon, Dee, and Wilson O' Leary. *A Guidebook for Cooperative Learning: Techniques for Creating More Effective Schools.* Holmes Beach, FL: Learning Publications, 1984.

This practical guide helps teachers implement cooperative learning in the classroom.

Feynman, Richard P. *Six Easy Pieces: Essentials of Physics Explained by Its Most Brilliant Teacher.* Reading, MA: Addison-Wesley, 1995.

Written for the general reader, this book is based on lectures by Richard P. Feynman (1918–88), recognized as a remarkably effective educator and as the most creative physicist of the post-World War II period. Feynman's clear, direct style introduces readers to atoms, basic physics, the relationship of physics to other topics, energy, gravitation, and quantum force.

Franck, Irene M., and David M. Brownstone. *Scientists and Technologists.* Work throughout History Series. New York: Facts on File, 1988.

> *Scientists and Technologists* looks at occupations associated with scientific research and innovation, including those of biologists, geologists, mathematicians, physicists, astronomers, and engineers. It explores how these occupations have changed throughout history and how they have shaped the world's civilizations.

International Technology Education Association. *Technology for All Americans: A Rationale and Structure for the Study of Technology.* Reston, VA: International Technology Education Association, 1996.

> This document is about how to develop technological literacy. It discusses the power and promise of technology; the process of technology; and how to integrate technology into the core of the curriculum, starting in kindergarten. You may also visit the ITEA home page on the World Wide Web (http://www.tmn.com/Organizations/Iris/ITEA.html).

Johnsey, Robert. *Problem Solving in School Science.* New York: Simon & Schuster, 1990.

> This handbook shows how to encourage children to think for themselves through a scientific approach to solving practical problems. It describes pupil-centered projects suitable for elementary students. Themes include elastic energy, seeds on the move, the measurement of time, wheels, and paper structures.

Johnson, David W., Roger T. Johnson, and Edythe Johnson Holubec. *Circles of Learning: Cooperation in the Classroom.* Alexandria, VA: Association for Supervision and Curriculum Development, 1984.

> This book presents the case for cooperative learning in a concise and readable form. It reviews the research, outlines implementation strategies, and answers many questions.

Krauss, Lawrence M. *Fear of Physics: A Guide for the Perplexed.* New York: Basic Books, 1993.

> The author is an internationally known theoretical physicist who shows how simple ideas at the heart of physics can be built on to develop the theories that drive modern research. Suitable for the general reader, this book does not discuss facts and theories of physics but illustrates how physicists think.

Micklus, C. Samuel. *Odyssey of the Mind: Problems to Develop Creativity.* Glassboro, NJ: Creative Competitions, 1984.

> The Odyssey of the Mind (OM) competition outlined in this book challenges participants to think creatively. The book presents a series of both long- and short-term creative problems and offers suggestions on how to set up and organize teams for problem-solving competitions. In addition to problem-solving exercises, the book includes information on team building, team selections, solving long-range problems, organizing OM competitions, and coaching OM competitions.

Taylor, Beverly A. P., James Poth, and Dwight J. Portman. *Teaching Physics with Toys: Activities for Grades K–9.* Blue Ridge Summit, PA: TAB Books, 1995.

> More than 700 educators helped develop the activities in this book. Grouped by grade level, the activities employ everyday experiences and toys, such as balloons, balls, and small race cars, to motivate students and help them develop scientific skills. Subject areas covered include acceleration, density, the electric motor, force, and gravity.

U.S. Patent and Trademark Office. *The Inventive Thinking Curriculum Project.* Project XL. Washington, DC: U.S. Patent and Trademark Office, 1990.

> This teacher's guide, available free of charge from the U.S. Patent and Trademark Office, can be used across all disciplines and grade levels. It encourages students to develop their creative potential and to synthesize and apply knowledge and skills by creating an invention or innovation to solve a problem. It includes 12 activities.

Webb, Colin. *Science and Technology by Design: 3.* Sydney, Australia: Harcourt Brace Jovanovich, 1992.

> This book contains nearly 100 activities that involve students in investigating, designing, and making things and using technology. The two-page activities are organized into 10 units. In three units, for example, students design and calibrate simple measuring instruments; investigate space; and investigate the use of levers, wheels, gears, and pulleys performing design tasks. Notes for the teacher explain the science concepts involved.

Williams, Pat, and David Jinks. *Design Technology 5–12.* Philadelphia: Falmer Press, 1985.

> This book seeks to establish the place of technology in the elementary curriculum. It offers teachers techniques through which they can explore a wide range of technological principles.

Resources for Students

Physical Science

Challoner, Jack. *Energy.* Eyewitness Science Series. New York: Dorling Kindersley, 1993.

> This book explores where we can find energy and how we can make the most of it. "Is it possible to build a perpetual motion machine?" and "How is energy used in transportation?" are two of the many questions answered. Experiments and demonstrations are included.

Cobb, Vicki. *Why Doesn't the Earth Fall Up? and Other Not Such Dumb Questions about Motion.* New York: Dutton Children's Books, 1989.

> This book answers nine questions about motion, explaining Newton's laws of motion, gravity, centrifugal force, and other principles of movement.

Lafferty, Peter. *Force and Motion.* Eyewitness Science Series. New York: Dorling Kindersley, 1992.

> This richly illustrated volume explores the principles of force and motion and describes how they have been applied from ancient to modern times.

> Topics include wheels and axles, Galileo's science of motion, gravity, weight and mass, and friction.

Sauvain, Philip. *Motion.* The Way It Works Series. New York: New Discovery Books, 1992.

> This short book defines motion, describes different types of motion, and discusses how motion is used in bicycles, escalators, typewriters, and other kinds of machines.

White, Jack R. *The Hidden World of Forces.* New York: Dodd, Mead, 1987.

> This book discusses some of the forces at work in the universe, such as friction, gravitation, electromagnetism, and surface tension. Illustrative experiments are included.

Technology, Engineering, and Design

Ardley, Neil. *How Things Work: 100 Ways Parents and Kids Can Share the Secrets of Technology.* Pleasantville, NY: Reader's Digest Association, 1995.

> This guide to the world of machines and technology includes hands-on experiments for students and their families. Color photographs and step-by-step instructions accompany the activities, which require readily available materials. Among the book's sections are "The Basics of Machines," "Construction and Buildings," "Transport," and "Information Technology."

Beeson, Phillipa. *Mechanical Power: Practical Science Activities for Grades 4–6.* Power of Science Series. Mount Waverley, Victoria, Australia: Dellasta, 1992.

> In this collection of activities on the mechanics of machines and tools, students investigate pulleys, levers, gears, wheel-and-axle systems, inclined planes, and flywheels. Students demonstrate, for example, how wheel-and-axle systems reduce friction, and they design and build a machine that fulfills a new function or improves on an existing machine.

Bellville, Cheryl Walsh. *The Airplane Book.* Minneapolis, MN: Carolrhoda Books, 1991.

> Illustrated with historic and contemporary photographs, *The Airplane Book* highlights developments in airplane design over the past 100 years. It discusses the principles of flight, early aviation, and current design challenges.

Bortz, Fred. *Catastrophe! Great Engineering Failure—and Success.* Scientific American Mysteries of Science Series. Illustrated by Gary Tong. New York: Scientific American Books for Young Readers, 1995.

> This book discusses engineering failures and shows how engineers try to find and eliminate anything that can lead to failure in their designs.

Boyne, Walter J. *The Smithsonian Book of Flight for Young People.* New York: Macmillan, 1988.

> This illustrated history of aviation is a celebration of human flight and of the men and women who have been an integral part of its progress. It recounts the story of flight from its beginnings, through the World Wars with their rapid advances in aviation, to the record-breaking flight of the *Voyager.*

Brusic, Sharon A. *Kids and Technology: Mission 21. Student Handbooks: Level 2.* Albany, New York: Delmar, 1991.

> This series for young students was developed by the Mission 21 Project of the Technology Education Program at Virginia Polytechnic Institute and State University. Each of the four books—*Discovery, Machines, Community,* and *Connections*—covers a different aspect of technology. A teacher's edition of *Kids and Technology* is available.

Butterfield, Moira. *Record Breakers and Other Speed Machines.* Look Inside Cross-Sections Series. Illustrated by Chris Grigg and Keith Harmer. New York: Dorling Kindersley, 1995.

> This book contains colorful cross-sectional drawings that show the interior and exterior of 12 speed machines of different eras and kinds—ranging from tea clipper ships to dragsters, powerboats, and Indy cars. Brief text and simple, technical facts about each machine introduce young readers to the technology of these vehicles.

Butterfield, Moira. *Ships.* Look Inside Cross-Sections Series. Illustrated by Jonothan Potter. New York: Dorling Kindersley, 1994. [Spanish edition: Butterfield, Moira. *Descubre todos los secretos de un barco.* A Través de la Imagen Series. Translated by Gems Pascual. Barcelona: Ediciones B, 1995.]

> This book contains colorful cross-sectional drawings that show the interior and exterior of 10 ships, including the *Mayflower* and a transatlantic liner. Brief text and simple, technical facts about each vessel introduce young readers to the technology of ships.

Gunning, Thomas G. *Dream Cars.* Minneapolis, MN: Dillon Press, 1990.

> The author describes a variety of present-day experimental cars and tells how teams of designers and engineers can forecast the shape of future automobiles. The book also discusses vintage cars and how they influence future designs. Color photographs illustrate some of these unusual vehicles.

Horvatic, Anne. *Simple Machines.* Photographs by Stephen Bruner. New York: Dutton Children's Books, 1989.

> This book for students in grades 1–4 describes five simple machines—the lever, wheel, inclined plane, screw, and wedge—and explains how they work.

Johnstone, Michael. *Cars.* Look Inside Cross-Sections Series. Illustrated by Alan Austin. New York: Dorling Kindersley, 1994.

> This book contains colorful cross-sectional drawings that show the interior and exterior of 11 types of cars, from the Model T Ford to the Formula I race car. Brief text and simple, technical facts about each car introduce young readers to the technology of automobiles.

Johnstone, Michael. *Planes.* Look Inside Cross-Sections Series. Illustrated by Jonothan Potter. New York: Dorling Kindersley, 1995. [Spanish edition: Johnstone, Michael. *Descubre todos los secretos de un avión.* A Través de la Imagen Series. Translated by Gems Pascual. Barcelona: Ediciones B, 1995.]

> This book contains colorful cross-sectional drawings that show the interior and exterior of 11 types of airplanes, from the German Fokker used in World War I to the Concorde. Brief text and simple, technical facts about each plane introduce young readers to the technology of airplanes.

Kerrod, Robin. *How Things Work.* New York: Marshall Cavendish, 1990.

> *How Things Work* presents projects, activities, and experiments for exploring areas of technology such as the wheel and rocket.

Lord, Trevor. *Eyewitness Juniors: Amazing Bikes.* New York: Knopf, 1992.

> Part of a series of 24 books, this book provides a close-up look at the world's most amazing bikes. Questions answered include, for example, "Where are some tricycles pedaled by hand?" and "Which bicycle had to be mounted while it was moving?"

Macaulay, David. *The Way Things Work.* Boston: Houghton Mifflin, 1988.

> This extensively illustrated reference book for readers of all ages demonstrates how machines—from simple levers to computers—do what they do. It explains the scientific principles behind each machine. One of its four parts, the "Mechanics of Movement," includes sections on the inclined plane, levers, the wheel and axle, gears and belts, rotating wheels, and friction.

Morgan, Sally, and Adrian Morgan. *Technology in Action: Movement.* Designs in Science Series. New York: Facts on File, 1994.

> This book is part of a series designed to develop young readers' knowledge and understanding of the basic principles of movement, structures, energy, light, sound, materials, and water, using an integrated science approach. A central theme of the series is the close link between design in the natural world and design in modern technology.

Van Meter, Vicki, with Dan Gutman. *Taking Flight: My Story.* New York: Viking, 1995.

> Vicki Van Meter tells how she piloted a plane across the continent at age 12 and across the Atlantic Ocean when she was 14. Her book tells of the obstacles she had to overcome to realize her dreams and integrates related fields such as mathematics, science, geography, and meteorology.

Ward, Alan. *Machines at Work.* Project Science Series. New York: Franklin Watts, 1993.

> Simple activities and projects in this book for grades 3 through 5 provide an introduction to machines. Topics include levers, pulleys, ramps and screws, cranks, compound machines, work, force, and friction.

Wheat, Janis Knudsen. *Let's Go to the Moon.* Books for Young Explorers. Washington, DC: National Geographic Society, 1977.

> The color photographs and simple text in this book show and tell of the journeys of Apollo spaceships to the moon and back to Earth.

Wood, Robert W. *Science for Kids: 39 Easy Engineering Experiments.* Blue Ridge Summit, PA: TAB Books, 1992.

> A variety of experiments introduce students to basic ways in which we use engineering. Projects include making a wind tunnel, building a truss, and testing the action of friction under various conditions.

Zubrowski, Bernie. *Wheels at Work: Building and Experimenting with Models of Machines.* A Boston Children's Museum Activity Book. Illustrated by Roy Doty. New York: Morrow, 1986.

> This activity book presents background information and instructions for using readily available materials (milk cartons, tuna cans, and thread spools) to make models of machines such as pulleys, windlasses, and water wheels. Included for each model are a list of materials, step-by-step directions, experiments for testing the model's capability, and a discussion of what is happening as the model works.

Inventors and Inventions

Berliner, Don. *Before the Wright Brothers.* Minneapolis, MN: Lerner Publications, 1990.

> This book by an aviation and science writer describes the ideas and experiments that led to the first powered flight by the 1903 "Wright *Flyer.*" Historic photographs and illustrations enhance the text, which begins with a chapter on "The Dream of Flight." The volume then profiles the pioneers who worked to understand powered flight—sometimes risking life and limb in the process.

Caney, Steven. *Steven Caney's Invention Book.* New York: Workman Publishing, 1985.

> This handbook for the would-be inventor includes activities, a list of "contraptions" in need of invention, and the stories behind 35 existing inventions. Topics discussed include collecting tools and materials, planning, record keeping, building a model or prototype, naming the invention, and patenting and marketing an invention.

Gates, Phil. *Nature Got There First: Inventions Inspired by Nature.* New York: Kingfisher, 1995.

> Illustrated with photographs and prints, *Nature Got There First* presents and contrasts inventions from eight categories of technology—including building materials, building designs, and the shape of tools—with nature's designs.

Jones, Charlotte Foltz. *Mistakes That Worked.* New York: Doubleday, 1991.

> This books tells the stories behind 40 things or processes that were invented or named by accident, including the vulcanization of rubber and the Frisbee disk.

Karnes, Frances A., and Suzanne M. Bean. *Girls and Young Women Inventing: Twenty True Stories about Inventors Plus How You Can Be One Yourself.* Minneapolis: Free Spirit, 1995.

> Part One of this book, "Inventors and Their Inventions," presents the stories of 20 girls and young women and their inventions; Part Two, "How To Be an Inventor," describes the steps in going from an idea to a working invention; and Part Three, "For Further Inspiration," includes additional information to encourage readers as they begin the inventing process.

Mitchell, Barbara. *We'll Race You, Henry: A Story about Henry Ford.* Minneapolis, MN: Carolrhoda Books, 1986.

> In episodes from the life of Henry Ford, young readers discover the origins of one of the most popular cars of all time—the Model T. They also learn of the Model T's inventor, who loved mechanical things even as a child and who used his creativity, foresight, and determination to turn his ideas into reality.

Platt, Richard. *Smithsonian Visual Timeline of Inventions.* New York: Dorling Kindersley, 1994.

> This unique timeline features more than 400 inventions that have changed the world. The book shows, for example, what was happening in the world when the bicycle was invented and how the steam engine influenced industry and transportation during the nineteenth century.

Reynolds, Quentin. *The Wright Brothers: Pioneers of American Aviation.* New York: Random House Books for Young Readers, 1981.

> This biography of Orville and Wilbur Wright, the brothers from Ohio who built and flew the first airplane, tells that their mother taught them as children how to analyze problems and seek new solutions. As adults, the brothers followed their dreams until they showed the world that people could fly.

Computer Software and Videocassettes

Leonardo: The Inventor. Nanuet, NY: Future Vision Multimedia, 1995. CD-ROM disk, with three-dimensional glasses. Macintosh and IBM versions available.

> This program uses music, narration, movies, and animation to present a look at the life, world, and works of Leonardo da Vinci. One of the six sections of the program presents several examples of da Vinci's inventive genius in the categories of flight, water, music, civil engineering, and warfare. The inventions are the major focus of the program.

NOVA®. *Fast Cars.* Produced by Cambridge Studios for WGBH/Boston, in association with Sveriges TV. Boston, MA: WGBH Educational Foundation, 1995. Phone: 800-255-9424. Videocassette.

> This NOVA® production covers a seven-month period, beginning in November 1992, when the Rahal/Hogan Racing company designed and built an "Indy car," one of the fastest race cars in the world. The program discusses the design challenges and surprising failure of the endeavor. It includes footage from races and interviews with the driver and design team.

NOVA®. Fast Cars Modules. WGBH Video, PO Box 2284-9040, South Burlington, VT 05407-2284. Phone: 800-255-9424. Videocassettes.

> This four-part set of NOVA® instructional videos with a teacher's guide focuses on understanding cars as a means of understanding physics. The individual videos are entitled *The Invisible Forces of the Wind* (being at the controls of an Indy car demonstrates aerodynamics), *To Survive at High Velocity* (vectors show how "corners make the driver and the car"), *Test Day* (focuses on the complexity of race cars, shown by testing every variable on the track), and *A Racing Engine for the Indy 500* (two companies battle to harness energy to create power).

Walt Disney Co. *Powerful Forces.* Distributed by Buena Vista Home Video, 1995. Videocassette.

> Known for his lively and informative television series on science for young viewers, Bill Nye explores the forces behind motion in this 50-minute videocassette.

National Science Resources Center Advisory Board

Chairman

Joseph A. Miller, Jr., Chief Technology Officer and Senior Vice President for Research and Development, E. I. du Pont de Nemours and Company, Wilmington, DE

Members

Ann Bay, Director, Office of Elementary and Secondary Education, Smithsonian Institution, Washington, DC

DeAnna Banks Beane, Project Director, YouthALIVE, Association of Science-Technology Centers, Washington, DC

Fred P. Corson, Vice President and Director, Research and Development, The Dow Chemical Company, Midland, MI

Goéry Delacôte, Executive Director, The Exploratorium, San Francisco, CA

JoAnn E. DeMaria, Elementary School Teacher, Hutchison Elementary School, Herndon, VA

Peter Dow, Director of Education, Buffalo Museum of Science, Buffalo, NY

Hubert M. Dyasi, Director, The Workshop Center, City College School of Education (The City University of New York), New York, NY

Bernard S. Finn, Curator, Division of Information Technology and Society, National Museum of American History, Smithsonian Institution, Washington, DC

Robert M. Fitch, President, Fitch & Associates, Taos, NM

Jerry P. Gollub, John and Barbara Bush Professor in the Natural Sciences, Haverford College, Haverford, PA

Ana M. Guzmán, Vice President, Cypress Creek Campus and Institutional Campus Development, Austin Community College, Cedar Park, TX

Anders Hedberg, Director, Center for Science Education, Bristol-Myers Squibb Pharmaceutical Research Institute, Princeton, NJ

Richard Hinman, Senior Vice President (retired), Research and Development, Pfizer Inc., Groton, CT

David Jenkins, Associate Director for Interpretive Programs, National Zoological Park, Smithsonian Institution, Washington, DC

Mildred E. Jones, Educational Consultant, Baldwin, NY

John W. Layman, Director, Science Teaching Center, and Professor, Departments of Education and Physics, University of Maryland, College Park, MD

Leon Lederman, Chairman, Board of Trustees, Teachers Academy for Mathematics and Science, Chicago, IL, and Director Emeritus, Fermi National Accelerator Laboratory, Batavia, IL

Sarah A. Lindsey, Science Coordinator, Midland Public Schools, Midland, MI

Lynn Margulis, Distinguished University Professor, Department of Botany, University of Massachusetts, Amherst, MA

Theodore Maxwell, Senior Advisor for Science, National Air and Space Museum, Smithsonian Institution, Washington, DC

Mara Mayor, Director, The Smithsonian Associates, Smithsonian Institution, Washington, DC

John A. Moore, Professor Emeritus, Department of Biology, University of California, Riverside, CA

Carlo Parravano, Director, Merck Institute for Science Education, Rahway, NJ

Robert W. Ridky, Professor of Geology, University of Maryland, College Park, MD

Ruth O. Selig, Executive Officer for Programs, Office of the Provost, Smithsonian Institution, Washington, DC

Maxine F. Singer, President, Carnegie Institution of Washington, Washington, DC

Robert D. Sullivan, Assistant Director for Public Programs, National Museum of Natural History, Smithsonian Institution, Washington, DC

Gerald F. Wheeler, Executive Director, National Science Teachers Association, Arlington, VA

Richard L. White, Executive Vice President, Bayer Corporation, Pittsburgh, PA, and President of Fibers, Organics, and Rubber Division, and President and Chief Executive Officer, Bayer Rubber Inc., Canada

Paul H. Williams, Atwood Professor, Department of Plant Pathology, University of Wisconsin, Madison, WI

Karen L. Worth, Faculty, Wheelock College, and Senior Associate, Urban Elementary Science Project, Education Development Center, Newton, MA

Ex Officio Members

Roger Bybee, Executive Director, Center for Science, Mathematics, and Engineering Education, National Research Council, Washington, DC

E. William Colglazier, Executive Officer, National Academy of Sciences, Washington, DC

J. Dennis O'Connor, Provost, Smithsonian Institution, Washington, DC

Barbara Schneider, Executive Assistant for Programs, Office of the Provost, Smithsonian Institution, Washington, DC